HOW TO
Write a Children's Book
AND
Get It Published

THIRD EDITION

Barbara Seuling

WILEY

John Wiley & Sons, Inc.

*To Sue Alexander, who's been there from the beginning,
and for Miriam Altshuler, who saw it through its rebirth,
with love*

For general information about our other products and services, please contact our Customer Care Department within the United States at (800) 762-2974, outside the United States at (317) 572-3993 or fax (317) 572-4002.

Wiley also publishes its books in a variety of electronic formats. Some content that appears in print may not be available in electronic books. For more information about Wiley products, visit our web site at www.wiley.com.

Library of Congress Cataloging-in-Publication Data:

Seuling, Barbara.
    How to write a children's book and get it published / Barbara Seuling.—Rev. and expanded.
       p. cm.
    Includes bibliographical references and index.
    ISBN 0-471-67619-5 (paper)
       1. Children's literature—Authorship. 2. Children's literature—Authorship—Marketing. I. Title.
    PN147.5.S46   2004
    808.06′8—dc22

                                                    2004004691

Printed in the United States of America

10 9 8 7 6 5 4 3

CONTENTS

ACKNOWLEDGMENTS

There are many people responsible, directly or indirectly, for helping in the preparation of this revision: the many writers—some of whom have become highly respected children's writers—who have told me that my book helped them get a strong start; the publishers who responded to my request for reading copies of books; Sandy Asher, Sue Alexander, Cathy Nichols, Katherine Gleason, Paula Morrow, and Sara McGhee, for their advice and help in areas I know little about; students past and present who have made me look like a good teacher by their successes; my writers group, Bonnie Bryant, Miriam Cohen, Sandra Jordan, Ellen Levine, Peter Lerangis, Harry Mazer, Norma Fox Mazer, Fran Manushkin, and Marvin Terban, for their constant encouragement and support; Steve Mooser and Lin Oliver of the Society of Children's Book Writers and Illustrators, who make me proud to be associated with them and the organization; Kitt Allan, who enthusiastically supported this project and Mike Thompson, who gently guided it to completion; Winnette Glasgow, whose unfailing eagle eye helps me always to put my best foot forward; and Miriam Altshuler, whose steadfast faith in me makes all things possible. My deepest thanks to all.

INTRODUCTION

Do you want to write a children's book? Are you excited by the idea of writing for children and the possibility of being published, but not sure how to begin or where to send your material?

Perhaps you want to immortalize a long-loved story, made up to amuse your children, or to remember and preserve tales told to you by *your* elders, complete with details of lives and places that exist no more. Possibly you live or work with children on a daily basis—as a parent, teacher, or librarian—and after seeing and reading a great number of books want to try your hand at writing one of your own.

Whatever the reasons, writing for children has undeniable appeal and its own satisfactions—but how do you begin? What do you do to break through that mysterious barrier that seems to exist between an idea and a finished manuscript, or between writer and publisher?

In the five sections ahead, you will learn what to do with your ideas and ambition. First, you are guided to the world of children's books and publishing as preparation for your job as a writer; second, you are shown how to find and develop your ideas and to look at your work critically; third, you explore writing styles and techniques as you write for different age groups; fourth, you learn about markets and approaching agents and publishers with your work. In the fifth and final part, you learn what to expect when you find success, what it's like to work with an editor, the importance of agents and understanding contracts, and how to join the community of writers.

These insights and observations, from my own as well as others' experience, may help you avoid some of the difficulties met by most beginners. Perhaps I can help you to plot a novel, or turn flat, lifeless characters into flesh and blood, but you will learn the bigger lessons as you put your words on paper day after day, creating strong manuscripts that make the reader think, see, and feel.

Publishers are always in need of new material. If you can write and communicate with young readers and make a commitment to stick with it, you can work your way toward publication, where you will be among the most respected and genuinely contented writers I know—those who write for young people.

PART ONE

A Closer Look at Children's Books

A good book respects a child's intelligence, his pride, his dignity, and most of all his individuality and his capacity to become.

—JEAN KARL, *From Childhood to Childhood*

1

You, the Children's Book Writer ... Maybe

Defining Your Goals

Can you define your goals as a children's writer? What do you want to achieve? Be honest. Do you want to make a lot of money? Tell wonderful stories? Explain the mysteries of the universe to children? Become a better writer? Do something with your ideas? Quit your job and write children's books for a living? Become famous? Communicate in some significant way with a younger generation?

Writers write because they have something to say, to feel a sense of permanence, to explore their own abilities in communicating, or just because writing is fun. Whatever the reason, it is usually compelling. Writing is addictive.

First, figure out what your goals are. Then, examine yourself squarely to see how near you are to those goals.

Are you ready and willing to work hard? Are you open to being taught? (Being eager to learn is not the same thing.) Are you flexible in your attitudes, able to accept suggestion and withstand criticism? Is your desire to write for children strong enough for you to cope with time pressures, struggles with words, and rejections? Are you strongly motivated to succeed so you will stick with writing no matter how tough it gets?

Are you a good writer? We usually know by the time we reach adolescence whether we can write well; significant observers such as family members, teachers, and friends tell us, and we can usually measure ourselves to some degree against our peers. Most writers succeed because of three things: they have fresh and

5

exciting ideas that they want to share; they have mastered the writing craft; and they have a good command of the English language.

Can you work alone? If you have never worked in isolation, you may be surprised. With no one around for input or feedback, no voices, and no bodies moving around, you can feel pretty lonely. When I first began freelancing after many years in an office environment, I thought I would go out of my mind because of the lack of human sounds and movement. I finally hung a full-length mirror at the other end of the room, where my reflection seemed like another person working.

Do you want to write for children because it's easier than writing for adults? Children's books are not watered-down adult books. They demand certain abilities of their authors, not the least of which is being able to tap into the minds and souls of young people without intruding, and to project the voice of those young people to the reader. You, as an experienced adult, have to recall feelings, attitudes, and viewpoints of your early years so that you can write about children convincingly and objectively. Charlotte Zolotow, a retired editorial director of Harper Collins's Young Readers Department and well-known author of children's books, called it "a kind of double exposure"—being aware of something as an adult and remembering what it was like as a child.

Not all of us can write for children; some cultivate the ability with effort. We must constantly step back and wriggle into the skin of the child and run around in her shoes before writing, yet we must craft our language with grown-up care, creating excitement and color, giving the young reader much to absorb and digest. I believe at the heart of writing for children is the author's own attachment, or emotional connection, to a certain period in her youth, although a rare few can write for several age groups and in various categories. Rosemary Wells is one of those people. With equal strength and appeal she writes picture books for young children and fiction for older readers.

It is our choice to write for children; we do not resign ourselves to a subordinate publishing group. Madeleine L'Engle, who won the coveted Newbery Medal, the highest honor for achievement in children's writing, for her book *A Wrinkle in Time,* was once asked why she wrote books for children. She responded, "You have to write whatever book it is that wants to be written. And then, if it's going to be too difficult for grown-ups, you write it for children."

What have you read? When was the last time you read a children's book? You cannot be ready to write for children if you don't read what they read, or know what kind of books are being written for them these days. Who are the authors most popular with children and with the adults who buy and read books to children? Whose writing style do you like best? If you could spend a week with three children's book writers to learn all the tricks of the trade, whom would you choose?

GOBBLE UP BOOKS

If the answers to these questions do not come easily, or if your answers reflect that your reading of children's books stopped around twenty years ago, start reading. Gobble up all the books you can handle. It's okay to read books published when you were a child, but read those published recently, too. If you need help in choosing titles, there are some excellent book lists available in appendix IX.

Read old books and new ones, popular stories and literary classics, good books and bad ones. Choose stories from various genres: adventure stories, picture books, teen romances, mysteries, historical fiction, nonfiction, poetry, funny books, and contemporary stories. If the person next to you on the bus is reading a steamy adult bestseller while you are laughing over a funny story for middle graders about an eccentric couple who keeps penguins in their apartment, don't worry; you will get used to it. Soon you will be so absorbed in what you are reading that you will hardly notice anyone else on the bus (and you may even miss your stop). Besides, isn't it reassuring that a book like *Harriet the Spy* by Louise Fitzhugh, published in 1964, or *There's a Boy in the Girls' Bathroom* by Louis Sachar, published in 1987, is still in print and popular, while many adult bestsellers are forgotten in a year?

Sometimes you will like a book but feel that it is not right for children. Or you will find that you don't care for a book that others find funny or clever. Whose work represents most closely the work that you admire? Are you repeatedly drawn to the books of one publisher? Your attraction to one or three or even six is significant; you clearly recognize something in the books published by those houses that is especially right for you, and this kinship will probably lead you, one day, to submit your own manuscripts to them.

Dig deeper and deeper as you read, and pose difficult questions to yourself. Start with picture books. When does a picture book seem too long? How important are the illustrations in picture books? What makes *Goodnight Moon* or *Curious George* remain popular over the years?

Move up a notch to books for children just beginning to read on their own. How does Barbara Park, author of the *Junie B. Jones* books, hold the attention of the six-year-old who grew up on a steady diet of TV?

When you get to books for the middle grades, note how the subject matter and style increases in sophistication. Jack Gantos wrote about a boy on medication for mood swings in *Joey Pigza Swallowed the Key,* and Christopher Paul Curtis balanced serious subject matter with humor in *The Watsons Go to Birmingham— 1963.*

Young adult (YA) books are more popular than ever. Why do you suppose teenagers who are reading on an adult level choose to read these books? Why are so many of them, like Caroline Coman's *What Jamie Saw,* or Walter Dean Myers's *Shooter,* or Norma Fox Mazer's *When She Was Good,* considered "edgy"?

Not all YA novels are dark. What drew so many teenage girls to Ann Brashares's *The Sisterhood of the Traveling Pants,* the story of four girls who shared a pair of pants while they were separated over the summer, or Janet McDonald's *Twists and Turns,* a hopeful story with lively dialogue and humor about two "project girls" who start their own hair-braiding business?

What about sensitive subject matter? How have the finest children's authors handled anger in a child? Loneliness? Fear? Guilt? In *The Great Gilly Hopkins,* how does Katherine Paterson write about a child who has been abandoned by the mother she adores, and who is angry at the world, with a fair amount of humor and great compassion?

Studies like these will help to sharpen your critical sense, which will later enable you to judge your own work more effectively. At the same time, you will become much more aware of good writing.

Incidentally, don't avoid reading books that you don't like, at least for now, while you're studying. In the past you might have just put down a book that did not interest you. Now, examine why you wanted to put it down. You can learn a great deal from this critical look. Why did the author fail to sustain your interest? What could she have done to keep you turning the pages? Perhaps you will uncover a weakness in your own work as you detect it in someone else's writing and will be able to avoid that weakness in the future.

Are you up to date technologically? If not, you may be left behind. Publishers continue to move toward easier and faster methods of production. Some accept queries and manuscripts electronically, and quick communication by e-mail is often necessary in the editorial process. The Internet is invaluable in research. If you do not have a computer in your home, you will probably find one at the public library, where it's free, or at an Internet cafe, where you can plug in for an hourly fee.

What have you already accomplished toward becoming a children's book writer? Consider your educational background and outside interests. What was your favorite subject in school—English? psychology? history? What are your hobbies—playing the guitar? collecting antiques? running? making jewelry? What jobs have you had—mom? firefighter? teacher? babysitter? dog breeder? pilot? speech therapist? cheese maker? crossing guard? popcorn vendor? Any background gives you a closer look at some special area, its people, atmosphere, and peculiarities. Some may be especially helpful because of their relation to children or books, but all will give you insights into human behavior.

Life experiences are your training ground for writing. Anything you see and absorb now may one day be recalled for a location, a character, development in a relationship, a motivation, or a supportive detail. Your perception and judgments, based on a lifetime of knowledge and practice, will have a direct bearing on what you choose to write about, and how you write it.

Do you have the patience to learn, the stomach for criticism, and the tolerance for difficult times? Are you willing to wait as long as it takes until you are ready to be published, to learn the skills you need, and to put in the necessary time in order to gain insight and experience? And then, do you have the stamina to persist, undaunted, through many rejections, before your work is accepted? These, perhaps, are the most crucial issues to confront, for if you come up positive in every other way but have not allowed for the patience and foresight to train yourself or to be trained well, you will lose heart at your first rejection and go down defeated before you have had a chance. It happens to many people because they are not realistic about the necessary hard work and persistence that it takes for the success they are seeking.

SUGGESTIONS—CHAPTER 1

1. Check the book lists in appendix I and the books listed in appendix VIII, and the titles that follow these suggestions. Select two or three books that sound interesting and start reading.
2. Think about what you read. What stands out? Is the subject matter appealing? Are the characters interesting? Can you easily distinguish one character from another? Is the plot clear? Does the ending satisfy? If it is a picture book, what do you suppose the editor saw in the text to know it would make a good picture book?
3. Think of a life experience you have had that could serve as background material for a children's book.

BOOKS MENTIONED IN THIS CHAPTER
(IN ORDER OF APPEARANCE)

From Childhood to Childhood, Jean Karl
A Wrinkle in Time, Madeleine L'Engle
Harriet the Spy, Louise Fitzhugh
There's a Boy in the Girls' Bathroom, Louis Sachar
Goodnight Moon, Margaret Wise Brown
Curious George, H. A. Rey

Junie B. Jones, Barbara Park
Joey Pigza Swallowed the Key, Jack Gantos
The Watsons Go to Birmingham—1963, Christopher Paul Curtis
What Jamie Saw, Caroline Coman
Shooter, Walter Dean Myers
When She Was Good, Norma Fox Mazer
The Sisterhood of the Traveling Pants, Ann Brashares
Twists and Turns, Janet McDonald
The Great Gilly Hopkins, Katherine Paterson

2

What Is a Children's Book?

The Variety of Books Published Today

When you say "children's book," what pops into your mind? Do you have an image of a big, colorful picture book that you can read to a child sitting on your lap? Do you think of a fat mystery or an adventure book—perhaps a Nancy Drew or a Harry Potter story—that is perfect for a rainy summer afternoon? Or do you think of a how-to or a what's-that kind of book that shows you how to build your own science lab, or tells you that sharks grow two sets of teeth, or discloses where you can find buried treasure? Are children's books, to you, bits of fluff, cute little pastimes wrapped in a pretty package?

Chances are, no matter what your personal image of a children's book is, you are not thinking of any of the following:

- A picture book about a little girl visiting her father in prison
- A biography of Hitler
- A teen story about a girl who cuts herself
- A nonfiction picture book about poop. That's right. Poop.

All of these are real children's books and can be considered representative of the breadth of the current children's book market. Not everyone will find their cup of tea in this selection, but the fact that these books are in bookstores and on library shelves tells you something about where we are in the publishing of children's books today and the sophisticated tastes of young readers. It also tells you that the image of the "cute little book" for children is not accurate.

We are in the information age. As we read books that stretch our imaginations and tell us of other times and places, we also read about the family of humankind and the social issues that beset our age. There are many kinds of books for children, with a depth and scope never before imagined, so it is truly impossible to fix on only one kind when you discuss children's books. You can check this out by visiting any bookstore with a well-stocked children's department.

You are entering a field that is small enough to know intimately, yet is vast and diverse in its range. Although you may have one kind of book in mind that you want to write, it is important that you are aware of all types of books. You will need this knowledge in communicating with other writers and editors. Following is a brief rundown of the kinds of books published today. Note how one category often overlaps another.

BABY BOOKS (0 TO 15 MONTHS)

Many parents and educators believe that exposure to a wide choice of books practically from birth will have an influence on a child's healthy intellectual development. Thus, there has been a great surge in books produced for infants. These books are probably heard more than seen, as they are read to the baby over and over again (sometimes in utero!), often crooned at bedtime for a soothing transition into sleep. Many of these come from the oral tradition of nursery rhymes, lullabies, and simple lap games shared between reader and baby.

BOARD BOOKS (1 TO 3 YEARS)

These chunky books, with their heavy cardboard pages, are a practical way of introducing books to toddlers. Little fingers can handle them roughly, turning thick cardboard pages that cannot be easily destroyed. Made up mostly of bright pictures, with as few as twelve pages, and only a few words on each page, these books are popular with parents as well as small children.

Coming up with texts for board books is quite a challenge, given the spare use of words. It's clear that the success of board books is writing about the familiar, subjects close to home. The hard part is keeping to story structure, just as you would for older books. For this reason, you will find many board books dealing with concepts, rather than stories, although some authors manage to get to the heart of babyhood in tiny little stories that please toddlers. Study those listed in appendix VIII to learn from the pros.

Some of the most beloved picture books, like *Goodnight Moon* are now available in board book editions, and work well, but sometimes the streamlined versions of the original stories lose their vitality and charm. Make your own comparisons to see the difference.

PICTURE BOOKS—FICTION (2 TO 7 YEARS)

The term *picture books* traditionally encompasses all books written for children from babyhood to about age seven, with plenty of illustrations. As a genre, these books expose children to a wide variety of ideas that expand their knowledge of themselves and the world around them, and stimulate their imagination.

Once a book has been read to a child and he likes it, it becomes part of him. He will return to it many times, because it is familiar and comfortable, like a favorite stuffed toy. He will go back to it on his own, using the pictures to provide clues to the text if he cannot yet read it on his own. With the reinforcement provided by many readings, children begin to pick out words and "read" their favorite picture books.

Children from one to three years old are beginning to explore the world around them. Attention spans are short as toddlers zip from one activity to another, so books for them must be simple and compelling. Concepts such as the difference between big and small, or fast and slow, are presented, as well as alphabet or counting books and books that name familiar objects or animals. Stories may be about simple day-to-day experiences: going to bed, taking a bath, losing and finding a favorite teddy bear, or the arrival of a new baby brother or sister.

As children grow, so does their need for stronger stories. At around age four or five, children can handle stories that make them think, feel, and understand. They like solid characters and simple plots. Examine a few picture books with stories. Imagine them without the pictures, being read over the radio. The stories should stand on their own. Illustrations, however, add to a child's reading development and pleasure.

Characters in picture books can do far more than readers can: they can sail away to far-off places, or (in the guise of animals) drive cars, or even have homes of their own, where they are in charge. Some picture-book heroes may get into hilarious fun and mischief far beyond anything the reader is likely to experience. This is heady adventure for children who can't even go outside without a supervising adult. Children read for the vicarious pleasure of imagining someone else's life as their own—just as adults do. They look for characters and situations that leap off the page with excitement, and stories with beginnings, middles, and ends. You will learn which writers have mastered the art of writing picture books as you continue to read in this genre.

PICTURE BOOKS—NONFICTION
(2 TO 7 YEARS AND UP)

In recent years, baby nonfiction has become enormously popular. Difficult concepts are explained in simple terms, and illustrated in great detail for clarity. The text is kept to a minimum while the illustrations "explain" the complicated aspects of the subject. Some of these books are even useful to children in the upper elementary grades.

At the youngest level, there are books with just enough information to satisfy a child's curiosity: the names of animals, colors, and objects, for example. When children are a little older and can handle more detailed information, they prefer specifics to generalities: where animals live, how food gets to the market, or how a seed grows.

A five-year-old may enjoy a book showing pictures of different types of whales. That doesn't mean he wants to know all there is to know about whales. Never underestimate the eagerness of a five-year-old to have his questions answered, but don't expect him to appreciate a lengthy answer when a short one will do.

The format of the picture book, with equal emphasis on pictures and text, is ideal for certain subjects, particularly in the sciences. Children who are reading higher-level books may go back to an occasional picture book to understand basic concepts about a subject or to see details illustrated. Sidebars and humorous touches, like cartoon characters and dialogue balloons, might provide readers with additional insights.

PICTURE BOOKS FOR OLDER READERS (7 TO 12 YEARS)

Another recent development in publishing is the picture book for older children. In this golden age of the documentary in film and TV, it is not surprising to find strong visual accompaniment in books as well. These books are often beautifully designed, with illustrations, paintings, collages, and photographs accompanying the text. The visual experience often accelerates understanding of a subject, much as an article in *National Geographic* magazine will do, but never waters down the content of the book. Biographies of important people have been done in this manner, as well as books on scientific subjects, the arts, and historic events. Information is solidly presented, with more text than is found in younger-level picture books, written at the more sophisticated level of the older reader.

EASY-TO-READ BOOKS (5 TO 7 YEARS)

Books for children learning to read on their own are available in a variety of categories—history, science, biography, and fiction—and for different beginning reader levels. The type is large and there is a lot of white space on the page, so new readers have an easier time reading. Great care is taken to give these books a more mature look, distinct from picture books, although illustrations still appear on every spread. The books are often divided into sections or chapters. Their resemblance to books that are read by older children is part of their appeal to beginning readers.

EARLY CHAPTER BOOKS (7 TO 10 YEARS)

The term *chapter book* is misleading, as we have always had books with stories divided into chapters, but that term has come to mean something else. These are books for the child who has outgrown the simplicity of easy-to-read books, and is ready to handle more fully developed stories, but is not yet at ease with the complexity of traditional middle-grade fiction. Early chapter books are illustrated, and the text is featured more than, rather than equal to, the illustrations. Humor is often, but not always, the driving force of these books, and lots of action and dialogue are essential. Early chapter books range from short (48 pages) to over a hundred pages. What makes them easier to read and understand are their simple plots, numerous illustrations, short chapters (two or three pages per chapter is not uncommon), and larger type and leading.

MIDDLE-GRADE FICTION (8 TO 12 YEARS)

This wide span accommodates the hungriest readers, whose interests range from adventure and fantasy to family stories, history, horror, and silliness. This group needs action and a solid story with good tension and a logical development of events. Children of this age are reading *Harry Potter and the Sorcerer's Stone* on their own, as well as Jean Craighead George's survival story, *Julie of the Wolves,* and Christopher Paul Curtis's story of a boy looking for his father in *Bud, Not Buddy.* You can't cut corners or put anything over on these readers. They will question glitches in plot and logic or weak endings, and will even write letters to authors who disappoint them or to ask them why they did what they did with a story. They can also become devoted fans and will read every book an author has written if they really like the first one they've read.

This is also where true literature enters the lives of young readers. Although one can argue that there are true literary works to be found in books for the youngest readers (for example, *Goodnight Moon,* a brilliant book for a child barely out of his crib), the real appreciation of literature forms in these middle elementary years when the world is expanding rapidly and social contacts and relationships may be forever. Writers for this age group are among the most beloved in a reader's lifetime. While pictures sometimes enrich stories in middle-grade fiction, they are less important to the success of the story than in books for a younger child.

MIDDLE-GRADE NONFICTION (8 TO 12 YEARS)

The middle-grade reader has an enormous appetite for straight-forward information on all subjects, spreading far beyond the school curriculum. The child who, at five, is happy with a picture book of all kinds of whales and a little information on each, at nine is thirsty for knowledge. He may pick up a book on whales, but it has to tell him what kinds there are, where they live, what they look like, their eating behavior, migration patterns, how they reproduce, and what scientists make of the interesting sounds they produce.

The text must be lively and well organized, whether your subject is whales, a biography of George Washington, or the story of the space exploration of Mars. Concepts should be within the understanding and experience of the reader, but not made too simple. Assume the reader has little or no previous knowledge of the subject and explain new terms or ideas. Accuracy is essential; therefore research must be thorough, sources reliable, and facts double-checked. Pictorial material and good page design are essential to clarify subject matter.

TEENAGE OR YOUNG ADULT FICTION (12 YEARS AND UP)

More advanced in style and plot than fiction for younger readers, with more attention to character and detail, YA fiction, as it is called, deals with more complicated relationships, values, and emotions. Stories are similar to adult fiction, but the heroes and heroines are teenagers. Fiction for this age group shows more introspection, passion, and unusual behavior, and employs sophisticated methods of storytelling, such as flashbacks and alternating viewpoints, than does younger fiction. Subject matter ranges from screwball humor to deeply moving issues affecting young people.

Although teenagers can and do read adult books, YA fiction appeals to them because the age of the protagonist is more in line with their own. They plug in easily to stories about young people like themselves, with recognizable concerns and experiences. They are searching for the truth and won't settle for less, which explains the recent upsurge in tougher YA books that show life as it is, not how we wish it could be: stories with an edge. Much of this genre addresses teenage concerns of the everyday variety—love, romance, adventure, mystery, relationships, history, peer pressure, independence, death—but themes and emotions can match adult books in strength and passion.

TEENAGE OR YOUNG ADULT NONFICTION (12 YEARS AND UP)

Teenagers read adult books on all subjects, but there are some books in this category that satisfy their need for knowledge yet still relate to them as teenagers. Readers are now old enough to be stimulated to probe and understand major ideas such as art, religion, politics, and war, and are drawn to closer inspection of the subjects that interest them. Whether readers are going on to college, they will have to make their way in a highly technological world and deal with major social and political issues. This age group has a wide range of interests beyond the demands of school.

NOVELTY BOOKS

This category refers to books that involve some unusual design, such as miniature books in boxed sets; pop-up books designed by paper engineers; activity and shape books; books that open into toys; books that can be zipped, patted, scratched, and sniffed; or books that float in the bathtub. Some of these are produced by book publishers, others are manufactured by toy companies. All go under the name of "book" if they can be read in the traditional way.

POETRY

Poetry is popular with children of all ages. It is a form of writing that cuts through the excess to the essence of ideas, capturing thoughts in capsule form. Perhaps it is this zeroing in, this getting to the heart of the subject without fluff or pretense, that is so appealing to young people. Poetry is also easier to read by those with "page fright"; children often do not read books appropriate to their age level because of the density of the type. Poetry provides short lines and a lot of white space. (This is the same psychology that created easy-to-read books.) Some delightful anthologies abound that gather many poets and styles into one volume. Collections by individual authors, speaking about many things through one voice, are also enormously popular. And, of course, there are many picture books in verse.

PLAYS

Children are always eager to act out plays, but too few authors write plays that children can enjoy reading as well as performing. For some reason, most accomplished writers never think of writing plays for children, although there are several collections of plays written to be performed by adults for the young audience. However, few plays exist, intended to be read and enjoyed as literature but also to be performed by children using simple props.

You will surely think of still other categories of children's books. If your view of children's books is slightly shaken, don't be alarmed: the field has simply exploded since your parents were young readers, and expanded even more since you were a child. Most people who are not intimately involved with books every day are surprised at the range of books now available to young people.

It's heartening to know that, in spite of advances in technology, the book business grows and thrives; editors still try to satisfy the sense of wonder and delight in the youngest readers and the curiosity in older ones, and to maintain the trust of all readers by providing the finest writing available. It is not an exaggeration to say that some of the finest books of the past few decades have come from children's literature.

SUGGESTIONS—CHAPTER 2

1. Go to the bookstore and see how many different categories of books described in this chapter you can find.
2. Get a small notebook that you can tuck in a pocket or purse (or, if you prefer going high-tech, an electronic one) and carry it with you at all times. Keep one section for notes on

your readings: record the author, the illustrator, the publisher, and the year of publication for each book you read, plus something significant, positive or negative, about the book. In another section, jot down observations from life or flashes of good ideas for stories or physical characteristics or any quirks of behavior you may see that can be used in your writings. Use this notebook often, the way an artist uses a sketchbook.

Books Mentioned in This Chapter
(in order of appearance)

Visiting Day, Jacqueline Woodson, illustrated by James Ransome
The Life and Death of Adolf Hitler, James Cross Giblin
Cut, Patricia McCormick
Everybody Poops, Taro Gomi
Harry Potter and the Sorcerer's Stone, J. K. Rowling
Julie of the Wolves, Jean Craighead George
Bud, Not Buddy, Christopher Paul Curtis
Goodnight Moon, Margaret Wise Brown, illustrated by
    Clement Hurd

3

How to Become an Expert

Getting to Know Children's Books

It is sad but true that to get a work published, talent is not always enough. Many talented writers drop out of sight when the going gets rough. Often, they do not understand the publishing system, cannot bear the rejection letters, and are frustrated by the long wait for a decision. Those who meet the challenges with intelligence and determination are generally the ones who succeed.

Perhaps you have heard about someone whose first manuscript was accepted on its first submission to a publisher. Or perhaps you've read that a rock star or TV personality has published a children's book and you know he's had less training for it than you. Such things do happen, but those are the exceptions. Don't fret over it. The "overnight success" may have entailed years of research and many hours of writing, and rewriting. The celebrity book is going to sell thousands of books on the name recognition alone; most publishers cannot resist this easy avenue to publicity and income.

Chances are you fall into neither category. You will have to get published the hard way, learning your craft and following a plan to success. You will have to suffer the indignity of the slush pile. If your skin is thin and your ego bruises easily, or if you cannot accept rejection, this is not the field for you. You'll have to toughen up. Professional writers know that they will probably have their work rejected before a publisher takes it on. Many average six to ten rejections per book before a publisher makes an offer to buy it. Twenty-eight publishers rejected Dr. Seuss's *And to Think That I Saw It on Mulberry Street* before it found acceptance and fame. Some careers would never have begun had the creators given up after early rejection.

The trick is not to take it personally, although when you're starting out, vulnerable and pitifully short on self-confidence, that's easier said than done. Assuming your writing and presentation are of professional caliber, there might be any number of reasons for a rejection.

Not all publishers—even those who publish books solely for children—publish all kinds of children's books. Possibly, there is a policy not to publish picture books, and yours is a picture book, or maybe you sent fiction to a house that publishes only nonfiction. Some houses have a particular philosophy, and your manuscript may not have embraced it. For example, the publisher may specialize in multiculturalism and your book, while brilliant, displayed no aspect of that theme. You may choose an appropriate publisher, learn the name of the editor, then not take the trouble to find out how to spell her name correctly. If you cannot accomplish this simple task, agents and editors won't take you seriously.

Perhaps an editor liked your novel but has one with a similar theme already scheduled for her next list. Or your book on sea monsters might have fit beautifully in their ocean-history series, but the series ended. A rejection of your manuscript may mean, simply, that your work is not right for that particular publisher at that particular time.

Hiring an agent may simplify the search, but the job of finding an agent can be as hard as finding a publisher. You will read more about agents in part four of this book. Meanwhile, it is important to know how the system works and the role of the editor, who is still the person you must win over because he will champion your work at the publishing house.

You will hear that decisions are not personal, but don't believe it. Editors are human. They make it a point to be objective, operating above their own personal biases, yet who knows what's working on a subconscious level? If your manuscript deals with a teenage kidnapping and the editor's own child disappeared recently, you may, inadvertently, have happened onto an emotionally charged field. If you have sent a manuscript about a cute raccoon to an editor who was just bitten by one and had to go through a series of rabies shots, she may not see raccoons as cute and may turn down your story.

Editors do not generally comment on the manuscripts they return to you. There isn't time to do any more than jot a quick note, and some editors feel that even that is not a good idea, giving false hope to a writer. However, if an editor sees something in your style or your idea that he likes, he may indicate he'd like to see more work from you. Be sure to note such comments with your next submission to that editor. It is these tiny connections that build, ultimately, into real relationships and, hopefully, to acceptance of a manuscript that is a good fit.

If you succumb to disappointment early in the submission process, you will have a hard time keeping your manuscripts moving. Don't despair. There's no time for it. Meet the challenge. Mark your records accordingly and move on.

THE BUSINESS OF CHILDREN'S BOOKS

You need to know what experienced and skilled writers have learned over the years: that publishing is a business, and editors must react to material with the economics of that business always in mind. What suits one editor on a personal level may not suit the sales director, who knows that he will not be able to sell the book, or the editor-in-chief, who feels the book does not fit the publisher's image. An occasional book that does not sell well is not so bad; it happens in all publishing houses in spite of expectations, promotion, and so forth, and other books that sell well take up the slack. As with all businesses, from baseball teams to delicatessens, the publishers must sell their products—books—in order to stay in business.

Many publishing houses have editorial committees, composed of several key figures in the company who are involved in the sales and distribution of books, as well as those who are responsible for the acquisition and editorial direction of new books. In the end, although an editor may find a promising author whose manuscript he likes, an acquisition will probably be a team decision. A book is published if the company feels it can support it in the way of production, promotion, and sales, and make a profit on it.

In recent years, publishing houses have merged into larger companies. A publisher may buy other publishers in order to expand, then get bought in turn by a large corporation, possibly with only a vague connection to books. For example, Simon & Schuster, once a large and respected privately owned publisher, incorporated smaller houses like Atheneum, Charles Scribners' Sons, and Macmillan, and was then bought itself by Viacom, a superpower in the entertainment industry that owns Paramount Pictures, Blockbuster, and MTV among others.

To add to the complexity of the situation, many publishers have multiple imprints—books coming out under various subdivisions, each with its own specialty. These are often under editors' names, as in Margaret K. McElderry Books at Atheneum, or Joanna Cotler Books at HarperCollins, although some have their own interesting names, such as Chicken House at Scholastic, or Penguin's Young Adult imprint, Razorbill, which ties in to TV and other nonbook media. You will find these imprints under the various publishers' listings in *Children's Writer's and Illustrator's Market* and other directories.

Learning something about the business of children's books should be part of your training as a children's book writer. It can be a valuable tool in the long run. *Publishers Weekly,* a magazine of the publishing industry, and various Web sites (see appendix V) will give you the latest publishing news including trends, sales figures, major acquisitions, mergers, and so forth. Tap into one of these regularly to keep up with the industry.

STUDY THE PUBLISHERS

The next thing to do is to take a closer look at the publishers and their imprints. Learn who they are and what their books are like. You can do this in a number of ways. There are various directories of the publishing industry, printed and online, listing publishers and submission information for writers as well as contests, conferences, and other related information (see appendix IV).

To sell their new books, publishers use catalogs containing a physical description and summary of each book. You can write to publishers requesting their latest catalogs, or you can go online to the publishers' Web sites.

By studying catalogs, you can judge the character of a publishing house and the specialties of its imprints. It will soon be clear to you which publisher is seeking the new and different and which is hanging on to the traditional, which focuses on fiction and which publishes a majority of, or only, nonfiction. You will see where new authors appear regularly and which houses feature contemporary novels, mysteries, or romances. Most publishers do a variety of books for all ages, but within that very general framework you can see preferences and priorities.

BROWSE THE BOOKSTORES—ONLINE AND OFF

The truth is, you don't even have to leave your house today to see the latest books. You can find publishers' catalogs online, and find descriptions and reviews of books on the Web sites of the major online bookstores, such as Amazon.com. The experience of touching, smelling, and handling new books, however, is what appeals to us in a good bookstore or library. Some of us never get over the need to browse the bookshelves personally, no matter how convenient the Internet may be.

The public library is a good resource, but you may not find the latest books there. It can take months to order, catalog, and shelve the newest books. Depending on the library's budget, the book you want may not have been purchased at all. There are interlibrary loans, but it can take some time to locate and acquire the book you want. What you can find in the library, however, are the well-worn, best-loved books of previous years, and a great deal of nonfiction that never makes it to the bookstores. You can also take advantage of the experience of the children's librarian, who knows the needs of a whole community of young readers and has a picture of the reading tastes of children discovering and choosing their own books.

If it isn't too busy a day, ask the librarian some questions. What do the most avid readers like to read? Are there books for bilingual children? Do award-winning books move off the shelves faster than other books? When a child asks for a funny book, what does the librarian recommend? Do series books encourage kids to read more? When there are budget concerns, which books are the first to be eliminated from purchasing consideration? How does a librarian select the books to be purchased from among the thousands that are published each year? How many of them are actually read before purchase? What percentage of the budget is used for books and what percentage for nonbook materials, such as computers and software?

For the most recent books, any bookstore with a full, rich, up-to-date children's department is the place to go. This might be a mega-bookstore chain like Barnes & Noble, or an independent bookstore devoted entirely to children's books. Beware of the standard shopping mall chain stores or discount department stores that sell a few well-loved and durable classics but mostly cheap mass-produced books or publishers' overstock so they can offer "bargain books" to their customers. They do not represent the range and variety of books available for children.

Dedicated owners of independent bookstores, like Tina Moore of The Blue Marble in Fort Thomas, Kentucky, are passionate about their work and take pride in knowing their customers. Moore makes certain the people she hires know books, too, and keeps an inventory of thirty thousand titles, going far beyond the current best sellers. She hosts presentations by visiting authors and illustrators, holds special programs and story times for children and their families, and provides a search and order Web site that can be used to access over 1.5 million books in print. In one of the store's four distinct rooms is a re-creation of "The Great Green Room" from *Goodnight Moon,* the setting of the classic book by Margaret Wise Brown and illustrated by Clement Hurd.

Elizabeth Bluemle and Josie Leavitt, former school teachers, read and review the books they sell in their bookstore, The Flying Pig, in Charlotte, Vermont, and publish an online newsletter for their customers, enthusiastically pushing their favorite books. There are always authors and illustrators appearing at the bookstore as well as celebrations of new books, holidays, and special events.

Booksellers make it part of their service to create an appealing atmosphere for customers, whether it's to celebrate Junie B. Jones's birthday or to hear a local author read from her work. Perhaps there is a foreign-language section or bilingual story hour, or a story session for which children are invited to come in costume. A good bookstore is worth searching for.

Children's books are mostly purchased by adults—parents, librarians, teachers, and family friends—who make the book-buying decisions and control the purse strings. Books for children are big business. It isn't just a phenomenon like *Harry Potter* that sells; people want good books for their children and are willing to pay for them. After all, a $16.95 picture book often provides far greater value and lasts a lot longer than a more expensive plastic toy. However, the ultimate influence on the longevity of a book is still the child. This makes selling a children's book a double-barreled challenge: not only do you have to satisfy the child reader; you must please the grown-up reader and buyer as well.

REVIEW THE REVIEWERS

To find new books that might interest you or to learn something about the latest trends in publishing, read reviews of current children's books. The best sources of these are a handful of trade publications that can be found in most libraries, or by regular or online subscription: *The Horn Book Magazine, School Library Journal, Kirkus Reviews, Booklist,* and the *Bulletin of the Center for Children's Books.* The *New York Times* and other major newspapers and magazines offer reviews of new books on a regular basis, and periodically devote a section to children's books; browsing through them is especially informative. Other review sources serve local regions or a particular market, such as bookstores, libraries, or parents of young children. The major reviewers appear in appendix II.

THE CHILDREN'S BOOK COUNCIL

The Children's Book Council is composed of U.S. publishers and packagers of trade books for children and young adults. One of its purposes is to encourage the use and enjoyment of children's books. A list of its members, available online, without cost, includes each member's address, main phone number, principal staff members, publishing program description, and, in some cases, manuscript submissions guidelines. A visit to their Web site will provide you with an excellent introduction to children's book publishing, with information and articles that can start you off on the right path.

Browsing and reading in all the right places, you will be amazed at how much background information you can pick up and how good you will feel armed with this vast new knowledge. It will change you from being a passive observer to an involved participant and, ultimately, to an expert.

SUGGESTIONS—CHAPTER 3

1. Using one of the publishers' lists in appendix I, look up a publisher you think you'd like to know better. Find out what they have published recently, using any means at your disposal—regular mail, the Internet, library references, and so forth. Remember to send a self-addressed envelope and postage if you request material by mail.
2. Find and familiarize yourself with a copy of the *Horn Book Magazine* (your library should have it). It has articles related to children's books, and a major section of reviews of the latest children's books. What do you find most interesting in it?

BOOKS AND PUBLICATIONS
MENTIONED IN THIS CHAPTER
(IN ORDER OF APPEARANCE)

And to Think That I Saw It on Mulberry Street, Dr. Seuss
Children's Writer's and Illustrator's Market
Publishers Weekly
Goodnight Moon, Margaret Wise Brown
Harry Potter and the Sorcerer's Stone (and sequels),
    J. K. Rowling
Junie B. Jones, Barbara Park
The *Horn Book* magazine
School Library Journal
Kirkus Reviews
Booklist
Bulletin of the Center for Children's Books
New York Times

4

Lessons from the Past

A Short History of Children's Books

For those aspiring writers who have no knowledge of the development of children's books, this chapter will sketch some of the rich beginnings and important movements that have affected the way we perceive the children's book today.

The book written just for children—for their enjoyment—is commonplace today but is a relatively new development in literature. First, we had to learn as a society to allow ourselves the pleasure of expanding our minds and our vision and to trust that, in sharing tools of enrichment with our children, no harm would come to them. This came with difficulty after our Puritan beginnings and lasted through the restrictive Victorian era.

There were a few exceptions, among them John Newbery's *A Little Pretty Pocket-Book,* an entertaining mixture of poems, pictures, stories, and proverbs suitable for young children, published in England in 1744. Before that, illustrated versions of *Aesop's Fables* were available as early as 1484, and Charles Perrault's collection of *Fairy Tales* was published in France in 1697.

The picture got better in the nineteenth century. There was Edward Lear's *The Book of Nonsense,* Lewis Carroll's *Alice's Adventures in Wonderland* and *Through the Looking Glass,* a few picture books by Kate Greenaway *(Mother Goose)* and Randolph Caldecott *(The Three Jovial Huntsmen)* in England, and in Scotland, Robert Louis Stevenson's great adventure, *Treasure Island.* Denmark's Hans Christian Andersen produced fairy tales that became known around the world, and in Italy, Carlo Collodi's *The Adventures of Pinocchio: The Story of a Puppet* entertained children. In the United States, Mark Twain's *The Adventures of Huckleberry*

Finn, written for adults, was immediately snatched up by young readers, and Clement C. Moore wrote *A Visit from St. Nicholas* just for children.

Along with these few treasures came many dreary publications emphasizing the three R's, religious instruction, or the various virtues, often clothed in melodramatic tales of pious children. Children's stories had titles such as *Blind Arthur and His Sister Jane*, and *Be Brave When the Trial Comes*. Still, to the children of the time, having stories of their own, even preachy ones, must have been a thrill.

In 1873, Scribners in New York published a magazine just for children. It was packed with stories, poems, pictures, humor, puzzles, and games, and it was called *St. Nicholas Magazine*. Edited by Mary Mapes Dodge, an author with excellent taste and vision, *St. Nicholas* blossomed, drawing the finest writers of the day, among them Louisa May Alcott *(Little Women)*, L. Frank Baum, (the *Oz* books), Rudyard Kipling *(The Jungle Book)*, Frances Hodgson Burnett *(The Secret Garden)*, and Joel Chandler Harris *(Uncle Remus* stories). *St. Nicholas* was the true forerunner of children's publishing in the United States. It was not until 1919, however, that Macmillan opened the first children's book department; others followed shortly after.

In the 1930s, children's books belonged to the illustrators. It was the time of Ludwig Bemelmans *(Madeline)*, Wanda Gag *(Millions of Cats)*, Kurt Wiese *(The Story of Ping)*, Robert Lawson *(The Story of Ferdinand* by Munro Leaf), and James Daugherty *(Andy and the Lion)*. It is no wonder the Caldecott Medal, for the most distinctive American picture book for children, was instituted at this time.

By the 1940s, the emphasis had shifted from picture books to longer stories. From that period came *The Moffats* by Eleanor Estes, *Rabbit Hill* by Robert Lawson, *Homer Price* by Robert McCloskey, *Charlotte's Web* by E. B. White, and Marguerite Henry's horse stories, including *King of the Wind*. Imaginations were wide open, and children explored colorful, magical, mysterious otherworlds through books, stretching their minds and their dreams, but always with the warm reassurance that everything came out right in the end.

A visit to the library today will show just how solid those books were—and still are. Many of them are still popular, worn and dog-eared with use. Picture books, produced in black and white under the restrictions of Depression-era budgets, are still as appealing to children as the more elaborate full-color books produced in recent years. Many are in the fiftieth reprinting or have been reissued with new covers or redesigned in more modern styles. It is a short education in itself to look at these books, and understand the simple success of them—the essence of what is good in children's books.

The 1950s brought us Theodore Geisel, under the name Dr. Seuss, and a shy but imaginative Danish-American schoolteacher named Else Holmelund Minarik. Dr. Seuss had been around for years, captivating children with his wonderful silly rhymes and equally silly but charming pictures. The new wrinkle was a book that was especially created for the beginning reader, using words a first grader could recognize. Up to that time the only reading materials for an emerging reader were dreary school textbooks of the Dick-and-Jane variety. Using nonsense verse and hilarious pictures, Dr. Seuss's *The Cat in the Hat* created a marvelous mess (and cleaned it up again, to the relief of parents), all the while giving the brand-new reader a bit of fun and pleasure along with a new skill—reading—as textbooks rarely did.

At just about the same time that Dr. Seuss was writing *The Cat in the Hat,* Else Holmelund Minarik created *Little Bear* to meet the desperate need of her first-grade students to use their newly learned reading skills to read something on their own that was satisfying, not a school text but a "real" book, with a story. Minarik's book about a small bear who behaves much like any active six-year-old, inspired enthusiasm and confidence in the youngest readers.

The Cat in the Hat and *Little Bear* were both published in 1957, beginning a whole new genre of books for children. Both Seuss's and Minarik's styles were eagerly accepted by children and widely imitated in subsequent years by just about every publishing house with a children's department. Today, the easy-to-read book is a standard category in many publishing programs.

In the 1960s came a genius named Maurice Sendak. Sendak had begun his career in an apprenticeship role under the wing of

Ursula Nordstrom of Harper & Row. Nordstrom discovered him while he was decorating windows for F. A. O. Schwarz, the toy emporium on Fifth Avenue, and invited him to illustrate children's books. Some of his early works include Ruth Kraus's *A Hole Is to Dig*, Meindert de Jong's *The House of Sixty Fathers*, and the *Little Bear* books by Else Minarik. Eventually he wrote his own books, first *Kenny's Window*, and then four tiny books in a box called *The Nutshell Library*, which has been a best-selling item in children's book departments ever since. Still, it was not until 1963, when *Where the Wild Things Are* was published, that everyone sat up and took notice of Sendak's amazing talent.

This was a golden time for picture books—a technological peak. Color reproduction was better than it had ever been. Advances were made in the quality of paper used in book production, reproduction techniques, and even in the printing inks. The economy was healthy, and schools and public libraries all across the country were buying books in large numbers. The government fed money for additional book purchases into the systems, and print orders were high. Prices were stable, and for $3.95 or $4.95 you could buy a large, full-color picture book, clothbound under its paper dust jacket.

A study of books published over the decades of the twentieth century represent major changes that have taken place. Books published before World War II show us to be a young nation drawn to its own sources of pride and pain: history, families, small town life, the Depression, and heritage. During the period of World War II, patriotic themes ran high. In the era of civil rights, we were a nation obsessed by social issues long overlooked, and our books for young people explored human rights, sexual freedom, the drug culture, poverty, the establishment, and unpopular wars.

As the mores of our society stretched to accommodate the departure from the traditional family unit, children's books reflecting divorce, remarriage, and restructured families began to emerge. *Dear Mr. Henshaw*, by Beverly Cleary, is the story of a boy who misses his father and who writes to his favorite author about his troubles. In *Divorce Express*, Paula Danziger wrote about a teenage girl who must interrupt her life every weekend to commute to New York to see her dad.

You may also notice a change in the appearance of books in the 1970s. We were a country involved in war, this time in Vietnam, and our uncertain economy greatly increased the prices of paper, printing, and labor. Publishers had to find ways to keep prices down, so there was a visible change in the quality of bindings and use of color, two of the more expensive areas in book production. It is interesting to note that the 1982 Caldecott Medal for the most distinguished picture book went to Chris Van Allsburg for *Jumanji,* illustrated entirely in black and white. Children's book artists seem always to rise to the challenge of restrictions.

The population explosion of the 1980s caused publishers' lists to bulge and expand as babies from the latest baby boom began to grow and become readers. Also in the 1980s, America's educators adopted a Whole Language approach to teaching. The idea of this method is that a child learns by using all his language skills (reading, writing, listening, and thinking) at the same time, crossing over from one area of learning to another. One result of this approach was that basal readers and other textbooks, designed to pound in words and information, were replaced in the classroom with trade books. As children were exposed to excellent examples of good stories and fine writing, they not only learned to think and to write more clearly, but developed into interested, rather than reluctant, readers.

By the end of the twentieth century, writers' and publishers' tools had advanced remarkably. Computers were now in use everywhere. Color in picture books no longer had to be restricted. Not only could writers take advantage of word processors to smooth the writing process, but artists could use programs to create or enhance pictures.

If you want to make a career of writing for children, learn about some of the people and books that came before you. This is a cursory look at the history of children's books, lacking in detail. If you wish to know more, books on the history of children's literature can be found in appendix III.

SUGGESTIONS—CHAPTER 4

1. Find three or four books originally published in the 1930s or 1940s and another three or four that were published in the

last decade. Compare the qualities found in the first group with those found in the second.

2. Read one of the Newbery medal books (see appendix I) and analyze it for its relevance to the year in which it was published as well as the period in which it was set.

BOOKS MENTIONED IN THIS CHAPTER
(IN ORDER OF APPEARANCE)

A Little Pretty Pocket-Book, John Newbery

Aesop's Fables, many compilations available

Fairy Tales, Charles Perrault

The Book of Nonsense, Edward Lear

Alice's Adventures in Wonderland and *Through the Looking Glass*, Lewis Carroll

Mother Goose, Kate Greenaway

The Three Jovial Huntsmen, Randolph Caldecott

Treasure Island, Robert Louis Stevenson

Fairy Tales, Hans Christian Andersen

The Adventures of Pinocchio: The Story of a Puppet, Carlo Collodi

The Adventures of Huckleberry Finn, Mark Twain

A Visit from St. Nicholas, Clement C. Moore

Little Women, Louisa May Alcott

The Wonderful Wizard of Oz (and sequels), L. Frank Baum

The Jungle Book, Rudyard Kipling

The Secret Garden, Frances Hodgson Burnett

Uncle Remus: His Songs and Sayings, Joel Chandler Harris

Madeline, Ludwig Bemelmans

Millions of Cats, Wanda Gag

The Story of Ping, Kurt Wiese

The Story of Ferdinand, Munro Leaf, illustrated by Robert Lawson

Andy and the Lion, James Daugherty

The Moffats, Eleanor Estes

Rabbit Hill, Robert Lawson

Homer Price, Robert McCloskey

Charlotte's Web, E. B. White

King of the Wind, Marguerite Henry

The Cat In The Hat, Dr. Seuss
Little Bear, Else Holmelund Minarik, illustrated by
    Maurice Sendak
A Hole Is to Dig, Ruth Kraus, illustrated by Maurice Sendak
The House of Sixty Fathers, Meindert de Jong, illustrated by
    Maurice Sendak
Kenny's Window, Maurice Sendak
The Nutshell Library, Maurice Sendak
Where the Wild Things Are, Maurice Sendak
Dear Mr. Henshaw, Beverly Cleary
Divorce Express, Paula Danziger
Jumanji, Chris Van Allsburg

PART TWO

Developing Your Ideas

Like bees who by instinct go from flower to flower gathering honey, writers, merely by being alive, are constantly gathering ideas and impressions—their honey—which eventually will lodge somewhere in some book.

— ELEANOR ESTES, from a talk given in New York to a meeting of the International Reading Association

5

Where Did You Get That Idea?

How to Find Ideas and Work with Them

Writers seem to fall into two categories when it comes to ideas: those who are always looking for a good idea, and those who have so many ideas, they don't know which one to work on first.

Consider the first group. These writers have good ideas, but often forget or misplace them. If you are among this group then the first rule, and the most crucial one, is to carry a notebook— traditional or electronic—with you at all times. (This is the same one you started in chapter 2 for jottings on observations and criticism.) Set aside a section for "Ideas."

MAKE NOTES

Record ideas in your notebook as they come to you, whenever and wherever that may happen—for stories, characters, behavior, dialogue, titles, or anything else. Trusting that you will remember a good idea until you get home, to the office, or someplace else where you can settle down leads to about 99 percent loss of that idea. Writing it down, even in your own brand of shorthand, at least calls it to mind, and then you can fill in the rest. Draw on these thoughts, phrases, and ideas for your future work.

I was walking along a busy street in midtown Manhattan when a man passed by, carrying a large manila envelope. He was dressed in nondescript colors from his head to his ankles, but on his feet were the brightest blue shoes I had ever seen. They caught my attention and held it so completely that it was worth

A page of notes from my Ideas *notebook. A story was germinating. Scribbled notes made in haste can work themselves into your subconscious and, eventually, into your work. This became "A Day at Coney Island," illustrated by Hilary Knight and published by* Cricket *magazine.*

a note, which I made on the spot and still have. I have no idea where or when I will use that character or detail, but someday I am certain that the little man in bright blue shoes with the mysterious package will appear in a story or scene.

I know someone who had great ideas falling asleep each night but found she had lost them all by the time she awoke in the morning. She put a pencil by her bedside, and in the dark, without disturbing her thoughts, scribbled a few words in tiny script on the wall beside her bed as the ideas came to her. It was brutal on her walls, but she had the right idea about hanging on to those good ideas.

Let your notes run free, and use all forms of writing—dialogue, prose, verse, sayings, phrases, slang—whatever helps you remember. Reminders like these, even in fragments, are a way of training yourself to see with a new perspective, to be alert to all the possibilities around you, to cultivate your power of observation and to hone your ability to absorb detail and store it.

Keeping a journal can be useful to your writing as well as a fascinating personal experience. Just as the artist's sketchbook shows her growth from year to year, so will your journal show yours. At the same time, the events in your life will provide a vital resource from which you can draw when you need authentic detail to bolster your writing.

Look for something new in the familiar. Perhaps it is the old vase Granny gave you seventeen years ago that sits on the mantel. Did you ever wonder where she got it? Did you ever really look at the design painted on it? Whose initials are those on the bottom? Choose something that you see every day. Look at it more closely than usual. It can be a tree in the front yard, your toothbrush, or the microwave oven. Think about how you might use that object in a story.

As you walk through your neighborhood, look around you. Can you tell something about the people who live in the houses you pass from the color and style of their blinds or curtains? Look at the geranium perched on the windowsill: who do you suppose put it there? An old woman? A young man? A person who misses a garden somewhere? Try to imagine what goes on behind one of the windows in your neighborhood.

CLIPPINGS

Another way to urge ideas to the surface is to keep yourself open to all forms of communication, from news items and magazine articles to TV programs, e-mails, cereal ads, computer games, overheard conversations, and theater posters. Collect pictures and clip articles. Look for plot ideas, characters, mysteries, settings, colors, and subjects for study and research.

Many writers create whole books out of small news items that just give the most superficial details of a deeper story. In my files, I have these: "Library Cat Is Out, and So Is Library," about a library that got written out of an old lady's will because it evicted a cat that had made its home among the books; and "Five Years after Kidnapping, Girl Celebrates 10th Birthday at Home." Look at the possibilities in these! What could the circumstances have been that took a child from her home at the age of five and then sent her back? What were those five years like? Who were her friends? Did she have memories of her home and parents? As clippings creep into the file, ideas begin to gnaw at you and grow. You never know when one of these ideas will work its way out of the file and into your creative bloodstream.

Use Your Own Experiences

An extraordinary source of material comes from your own experience. Since you write about and for children, move back in time to when you were a child. Think back on how you felt when your brother or sister got something you wanted; or when you wished your dad would come and tuck you in; or what it was like when your mom and dad had an argument, or took you to a ball game. What was it like when your mom read you a story; did you speak up in school or were you shy? What made you cry? What did you think about the whole Santa Claus thing, or ghosts? Remember your first day at a new school, your first best friend, and how it felt to wear a new pair of shoes or share something with someone you didn't like? Work at it. Recall a nasty grown-up, what your room smelled like, how a piece of bubble gum tasted, a game you invented with your brother.

Try to remember what it felt like in these different situations. These are the truest feelings you can write about because you know them intimately. The apartment in Brooklyn in which I grew up is the background for one story of mine; in another I use Coney Island and the boardwalk, scenes of my own past, to underscore the atmosphere. One of my short stories involves a boy who has to take off some weight, a problem close to my heart, and a second is about tagging along with an older brother, again a situation I remember well.

If you have trouble remembering, put together scattered thoughts or memories until you have pieced together a whole episode. Go through a family album and try to remember the background for a photo. What time of day was it? How did you feel about the other people in the picture? Where was the picture taken? How old were you? Where did you get the sweater or baseball cap you wore in that picture?

The more you work at piecing together the clues you see before you, the more you will evoke whole episodes and flavors and feelings. Maybe playing music from that period will help you to make associations. Eventually, you can draw on this personal treasury even when the places in the photographs have ceased to exist.

You can make up anything you like when you're writing fiction, but at the core of it will always be your own experiences, what you observed, and how you felt about things when you were a child.

BORROW IDEAS FROM OTHERS

Author Jean Fritz, whose memorable biographies of famous people have entertained young readers for decades, once said that because she did a lot of running back and forth across the time zones in her life, she liked reading about the childhoods of others, to see how they did on their journeys. That's one way to stimulate ideas: curiosity. There are others, equally inspiring. As you read more children's books, try to see how the ideas for stories evolved. Read something about the authors; do a bit of research. You may also pick up ideas for yourself as you read about other people and their books. Within each story there are a dozen other stories floating around, waiting to be snatched up. A story about a foster child may remind you of a classmate you once knew who lived with her grandmother; the grandmother may have been quite a colorful character in her own right. Could she be a figure in your next story? One thing leads to another, and it can go on and on, a network of good ideas. Be open to it and willing to stretch a bit to look in all the corners; the possibilities are endless.

One way to meet the challenge of coming up with new material and new ideas in spite of all that has been done before is to take an old theme and try to improve it, cultivate it, give it more depth and meaning. In doing this you will make it your own, and for the time being, it will save you the trouble of coming up with a brand-new idea. Think of what Arthur Laurents accomplished when he took the theme from Shakespeare's *Romeo and Juliet* (1594) and created the book for the contemporary classic musical, *West Side Story* (1957). And, if you dig a little deeper, you'll find that even Shakespeare borrowed his theme, from a narrative poem by Arthur Brooke (1562).

FOCUS ON ONE IDEA

What happens if you are in that other group of writers—the one where ideas come like grains of sand in a desert windstorm and settle thickly on the pages of your notebook? You probably have lots of unfinished pieces around, and fat, bulging notebooks filled with loose notes. To stop being a note taker and become a writer, you must focus.

Commit. Choose one of your ideas by any means at all. If one is particularly timely, you might choose it for that reason. Pick one from a hat if you cannot decide. Take that one idea, roll around in it, and don't let it go until you can either feel the satisfaction of its completion or forget it forever. This may seem harsh, but if you are stuck in the mire of too many unformed and unfinished ideas, you must do something aggressive to get out. Sometimes you simply have to face that an idea is not as good as you thought it was and you should not waste more time on it. Sometimes, this force of discipline results in a completed piece; take the chance. If it helps, bring the work to a critique group to air it. However it turns out, you will start to unclutter your files and your mind. The feeling of accomplishment and freedom will enable you to move on to something else.

The important thing for the perpetual note taker is to get something done, finished to the point where she has devoted attention and time to it and given it a fair chance. Many aborted stories are the result of too many ideas crowding in at once, preventing any one of them from having breathing space, a chance to survive.

Maybe you don't have dozens of notebooks filled with half-done stories, but you've still got a problem with too many ideas; maybe all your ideas are still in your head. The same rule applies: focus. Get hold of your thoughts and put them on paper. Choose one idea and sketch it out. Don't labor over it; if you don't set out to do it perfectly, you will have a better chance at conquering your fears. Once the skeleton of the story is in place, it will be easier to find the courage to go on with it, to put flesh on the bones to do the polishing.

Since your aim is to finish a piece of work, it is important that you choose something relatively easy to work on, without complications. Avoid unnecessary barriers to success such as a piece that requires excessive research, or one with a really unusual character or theme. If an animal is the main character, choose a familiar animal rather than an uncommon one. The only thing you want to stand out right now is your writing, and the trappings should not detract from that.

Whatever you have to do to come up with an idea that works, remember that your ideas are only a starting place. It is in the telling of your story that you compete, and that is where your skill as a writer comes in, sets you apart, and makes the editor sit up and take notice.

BRAINSTORM

One of the most effective ways to get an idea working for you is to brainstorm. Jot down a key word or phrase with your basic idea. Radiating from that word, jot down words you associate with that phrase. As each associated idea comes to mind, jot it down. Soon you will have all kinds of spinoffs from those ideas all over the page, like the spokes in a wheel.

Play around with the associations and ask "What if . . . ?" What if your hero does this instead of that to solve the story problem? What if he decides to ignore the problem? What if, when things go really bad for him, his best friend isn't there for him? The possibilities are endless, but sooner or later, you will fix on something that is exciting for you, and you'll know that's the way you want to go with your idea.

SUGGESTIONS—CHAPTER 5

1. Choose a time when you are among strangers. Single out one person and observe how she sits, walks, talks, moves, wears her hair, or carries her briefcase; how she reads her newspaper; and so on. Look at her hands. What can you tell from looking at them? Give this person a background, a personal history. What might her occupation be? Her ethnic makeup? What do you suppose she would do if there were an emergency just when you are studying her? Make notes, and write up a character sketch later.
2. Clip an article from your readings in the next week that you think would make a good solid story for children. Write a paragraph outlining the story you could create based on this clipping.
3. Choose any one of these subjects to brainstorm. Play around with it until you find the idea that will help you develop it into a story.

    Practicing a musical instrument
    Stocking shelves in the supermarket
    Surfing the Internet
    Babysitting a brat
    Finding twenty dollars
    Writing a fan letter to your favorite rock star
    Being outside in an unexpected storm
    Waiting on a street corner

6

Sabotage Made Easy

Procrastination and What to Do about It

I am the worst procrastinator the writing craft has ever known. No sooner do I sit down at my desk to work than I remember that my friend's father is recovering from bypass surgery, so I should call to find out how he's doing, and that cousin Gloria's birthday is next week, so I ought to run out to the store and buy her a card so it reaches her in time.

If I am not careful to ignore these nagging ideas, no matter how insistent and worthwhile they are, the restlessness will build and finally I will get up from my chair. On the way to another room, I might notice that the dog needs more water or that the lightbulb went out in the living room and should be changed, so I rummage around looking for a new bulb and come across the tape measure, which reminds me that I should take the measurements for the bathroom wallpaper we've been talking about changing. And, while I'm interrupted anyway, I might as well run out to the supermarket, because we're almost out of milk.

There is no end to the problems you can create to keep yourself from writing. Uri Shulevitz calls these games we play "sabotage," guaranteed to mess up your most perfect plan for writing, if you let it.

ESTABLISH PRIORITIES

Of course, you have to put certain things above all else; the health and safety of your children, or your job that pays the rent, for example. Attempting to write with two active children running around is a clear invitation to sabotage; but there are times when the children sleep or are at school. And although you have a demanding job, you do not work morning, noon, and night. Your life as it is has to be examined and a plan made to work around your commitments. If you don't claim some sacred time for your writing, having great ideas for stories will not matter, because you'll never get to work them through.

After you sort out the necessary demands on your time, and you know that the time you have allowed for writing is not stolen from anything more important, you still have to deal with fear. You may be afraid of filling that blank page or screen with imperfect prose; of meeting the expectations of friends, family, or yourself; of success (can you handle it?); of failure (are you wasting your time?); afraid that, at best, your work will be mediocre. We may tell ourselves it's laziness or lack of motivation, but usually we are just afraid.

The truth is, all writers have fears because all writers are human. With some, the fears get in the way of writing. Successful writers are worried that they cannot top what they have already done, and so they avoid trying. Unsuccessful writers fear that they are failures because they have not been published and feed that fear by avoiding more writing, perpetuating the failure-to-publish syndrome. Many writers feel this at one time or another; the words just aren't as crisp and as witty on paper as they are in your head. You think, maybe I have nothing really interesting to say; if I wait and start tomorrow, maybe it will come out better. There is always some excuse. It takes courage to overcome fears, so start training yourself to work up the courage you will need time and again to write. If you wait around, hoping that something will happen to get you back on track, you are asking for defeat. Courage means pushing yourself to take that first scary step toward where you want to go, not waiting for rescue.

There are ways to avoid playing this sabotage game, which you can never win. First, you must look at your writing in terms of priorities. How important is writing to you? Look clearly at how you evaluate your interest in writing so that you will know how much to demand of yourself. If writing is about as important to you as building a birdhouse for the backyard or cooking a gourmet meal, then don't put any more pressure on yourself than you would in those activities. Give writing the same time you do those things, and move at your own pace. Write for enjoyment, but don't think about being published.

If writing is more important to you than anything, including family, health, or job, you are at the other extreme. You will not write to publish, either, but more to feed your passion and communicate with your muse, and you will not care if anyone else reads or likes what you write. If you are one of these writers, know that it will be difficult to maintain a family or social life while you write. Yours will be an eccentric situation, at best, and perhaps you ought to make some arrangements with your loved ones before you seal yourself off to work so that you can be reached in emergencies, have the children cared for, and so on. You probably won't have the patience to study methodically, but will surface to consult reference material from time to time.

If you are in between these two positions, you will most likely work out a system to incorporate writing into your life so that you can learn at a steady pace and have the time and space to grow as a writer. You must give writing at least the same attention that you would any on-the-job training program, because that is what this is: training for your future as a writer. That means making room for it in your already busy schedule, for if you do not allow yourself the time and treat writing with a sense of importance, you will never become any kind of writer.

If you are worried that you may not be suited for children's writing, or that you won't be any good at it, relax. Give yourself the chance to find out. Only after you do the work and study and practice for a reasonable length of time will you be able to assess your abilities and decide if writing for children is what you really want. Then, if you wish to spend more of your time and creative energy in this pursuit, you will have a better idea of what is required to accomplish your purpose.

Your life is 100 percent full now, so how do you make space for something new? Consider that you have made room before, for jogging or a computer course or meditation or doing your aerobic workout in front of the TV. You know that you can always squeeze in fifteen minutes a day, so start with that. Fifteen minutes should not turn your life upside down and can get you started on a very important course. Right now you are at the beginning of a brand new discipline, and setting up regular work habits is far more important than the length of time you spend at it.

WRITE EVERY DAY

For the next two weeks, you must write for at least fifteen minutes each day—and no days off. Those minutes must be good, fresh, energy-rich minutes, not "leftovers" from the day. Don't wait until eleven o'clock at night and try to cram in your writing before you go to bed. You are too tired then, and your head is too full of the day's activities and problems. Pick a fresh, uncluttered time. Perhaps it will be before everyone else gets up in the morning. Maybe you will find lunchtime, when the office or house is quiet and the phone is not ringing, the ideal time. If you must use the later part of the day, clear your head and lungs and get your blood full of oxygen by taking a walk or doing some deep-breathing exercises before you begin to write. Any time that is truly yours will work fine.

When you sit down to write, do nothing else. Don't look for your special shirt or magic pencil; one day you will be without them and you will be on your own, without lucky charms to help you. Write anything, as long as it is creative: forget grocery lists, journal entries, and letters. Write stories or parts of stories, character sketches or bits of dialogue between two fictional characters; describe places, objects, or feelings. Try telling a story from the point of view of two different children or from an adult and a child's viewpoint, without using adjectives. Imagine yourself at age seven going to sleep in a strange place, being afraid of the dark, and inventing ways to get your mom or your Aunt Lydia to come into your room. Think back on what it was like to have a grasshopper in your fist or a giant jawbreaker in your mouth, or what it felt like when your best friend found a new friend and left you out.

GETTING STARTED

If you get the cold sweats as you begin, copy a few passages from a favorite book. (This is an excellent exercise, by the way; it gives you insights into other writers' use of structure and form.) Just don't get carried away; this is only a warm-up.

There are endless ways to use this time. You don't have to complete a story or even have a story idea ready each time you sit down. Bits and pieces add up and can be useful in later writings. They help you to create a world for your story. They are your sketchbook, your training in observation.

If you think everything you write is junk and it depresses you to have it lying around, throw it away. Why torture yourself? This is practice, and you don't have to show your work to anyone. Toss things in the wastepaper basket, and remember to empty it at the end of the day. Leave no traces. Start fresh each day. Eventually, you will want to hang on to something, and then something else, and, as your confidence grows, so will your file of writings.

WRITE REGULARLY

As you do more writing, and can handle your fifteen minutes with ease, you can stretch the time to longer and longer periods. Be careful not to be overzealous and take on more than you can do, or you will quit in despair one day and defeat the purpose of the exercise. It is important to remember that regular periods of writing each day, no matter how short, are more important in the long run than spending several hours in a row writing on weekends. Perhaps you will do both, but if you have to give up one, cancel the weekend sessions and hang on to your daily discipline, at least for now. The weekend writer has to contend with revving himself up to the task, which can waste plenty of time. Your regular routine will get you so used to writing that eventually you will need only seconds to get in the swing when you sit down to work.

Sometimes the format of tidy chapters or sections creates its own set of problems for the writer. If you are writing a long book and have trouble with beginnings, resist the temptation to finish things off neatly each day. Stop before you finish a chapter. You can jump into the middle next time and not have to face a new beginning. Chances are, once you have picked up momentum, you will go right into the next section as you finish the present one.

How Much Time Should I Spend on Writing Each Day?

There is no set plan that you have to put in a specified number of hours each day at your writing. Each of us has individual needs and tolerances. Jean Rikhoff told a group of writers at a conference I attended some years ago that she worked on her adult novels for one hour a day—never more than two—and in that time, she had to produce one page. That guaranteed more than three hundred pages a year. Walter Dean Myers, well known for his gutsy young adult novels, works to a quota; he must produce ten pages each day, no matter how long it takes.

I spend about four or five hours a day writing, and the rest of the day on other matters related to my work. That doesn't mean I haven't tried every system imaginable. At one time, my work plan changed from book to book: so many days per chapter, so many hours per day, writing on alternate days. If I read of an admired writer's work schedule or method, I tried that. I kept logs, recording my hours and/or pages in a notebook. Sometimes I would hit a snag and go over the allotted time, and at other times I finished way ahead of schedule and got an afternoon off. However, the apportionment of time helped me to produce regularly and to meet deadlines. You will find your own system and tolerances, making adjustments until you find what works for you.

Build Up Your Concentration

Concentration is crucial when you write. It is important not only to maintain your thoughts but to keep yourself from wasting valuable time. If you have a problem concentrating, try to work out ways to improve your attention span. When you sit down to write, what are your main distractions? Keep a pad nearby and jot them down for an entire day. Then take a look at your list and see what you can do to make the necessary changes to eliminate the biggest distractions.

Is it too noisy? Wear earplugs if they help. Perhaps you need to work in some other, quieter, place. Is there a part of the house you can close off while you work? Perhaps a friend will let you use his office or house during a part of the day when he is not there.

Or try working at the library. Christopher Paul Curtis wrote his first book, *The Watsons Go to Birmingham—1963*, a Newbery Honor book, as well as *Bud, Not Buddy,* which won the coveted medal, at a table in his local library. Some libraries have computers and offer free access to the Internet, should you need to do some research while you're at it.

Is it too quiet? Try working with the radio or tapes playing softly in the background. Some writers find that recordings of waves flowing or tree leaves rustling, or certain classical music, dulls other sounds and provides a relaxed atmosphere. The music you play should not be the kind that makes you hum or tap your foot or in any way interferes with your thinking.

Can you work by yourself or must you have other people around? Does it help to have your dog in the room or should you keep him outside while you work? Most distractions can be overcome if you are willing to examine your behavior and make some necessary changes.

SHAKE OUT THOSE KINKS

Pain or discomfort from sitting too long in one position or staring at a computer screen without a break can be a problem. Looking at the computer screen over a prolonged period of time can cause severe eyestrain. I solved this problem by getting a second pair of eyeglasses that are just right for the distance between my eyes and the computer screen, but not for much else. They stay next to my computer when I'm not wearing them. The simple exercises outlined on these pages can also help.

If you have pains shooting through your wrists and fingers, it could be from the compression of nerves in your wrist due to the swelling of tendons—a result of overuse commonly known as carpal tunnel syndrome. For relief, you can wear a simple wrist brace, available at most drugstores, or purchase a special ergonomic pad on which to rest your wrists while typing to keep them from bending at the point of compression. For any keyboard activity, frequent breaks are recommended. Do other related chores during these breaks that do not use the same repetitive motion used in typing. If pain persists, however, you may need to see an orthopedist. Whatever the problem, identify it and work it out before you have a serious condition.

1. EXERCISES FOR BLURRY EYES

Sit in the middle of a room and look as far to your left as you can without moving your head or turning your body. Move your eyes clockwise, pausing at 12, 3, 6, and 9 o'clock. Repeat this several times. Then do the same thing in the opposite direction.

2. EXERCISE FOR FOCUSING YOUR EYES

Focus on something far away, like a sign. Hold a book in your hands about fifteen inches away from your face. Look at the sign and concentrate until you have it in focus. Then look at the book, concentrating on it until the words are in focus. Spend two minutes alternating your gaze between the sign and the book.

After several hours at the word processor, your eyes can show signs of strain. At such times, it helps to exercise your eyes, particularly the focusing muscles.

If you get stiff sitting too long at your desk, get up from your chair for a break now and then and do a few stretches; these are good for your back, neck, and shoulders, the main problem areas for writers.

After many years of giving in to sabotage, I have learned to work in my home successfully by exercising frequently near my desk and by keeping a coffeepot nearby so that I don't have the excuse of going to the kitchen several times in one morning. I also have a telephone answering machine that is switched on during my work hours; it collects messages for me, and I deal with them when I am on a break or have finished my writing for the day.

If after all these tricks you still suffer from distractions, you will have to work at building up your concentration bit by bit. One way is to listen to a piece of classical music through to the end without falling asleep or tidying up the coffee table or doing anything else. Learn to listen, to identify the different musical instruments, to follow how the composer uses his theme through-

---

EXERCISES FOR NECK AND SHOULDER STRAIN

1. Every twenty minutes or so, stand up at your desk. With your hands at your sides, raise and lower your shoulders ten times.
2. Keeping your hands at your sides, rotate your shoulders, first forward ten times, then backward.
3. Roll your head around as far as it will go, first to the left, then to the right. Repeat ten times in each direction.

Working for long periods at your desk or at a computer can put quite a strain on your neck and shoulders. These simple exercises can ease some of the tension.

out the work. Practice this for a while. Apply it to reading; read as many pages as you can (for pleasure) before you are distracted or find yourself rereading whole passages. Time yourself. Aim for more pages in the same amount of time. Keep at this until you have built up your period of concentration to at least four times its previous length.

As you succeed in the music and reading exercises, work at improving your period of concentration as you write. Refuse to get up from your desk until a certain amount of time has passed. Get tougher on yourself. Stretch out the period a little longer. As you increase your time, give yourself several days, or even weeks, to get used to the new time schedule before pushing too hard for more.

GOOFING OFF

Once you have established how important writing is to you and have worked out a time plan and a method of sticking to your work, allow yourself plenty of goof-off time. This may seem counterproductive, but it is not. As a matter of fact, goofing off is essential to your success. It is how I learned to live with my propensity for sabotage as well as my tendency to be a workaholic, and you can learn it, too. You must have some time each day to make phone calls, run, water the plants, read the stock market report, bake a pie, sharpen your pencils, practice the piano, do a crossword puzzle, play with the kids, walk the dog, watch a DVD, or take a nap. Even if you do nothing in your goof-off time, take it anyway. If you don't have this outlet for the day-to-day "fillers" in your life, they will intrude at the worst possible moment, during your writing time, and interfere with your concentration.

Set limits. Goof-off time should not spill over into time allotted for anything else. Give it an hour, a morning, whatever you feel is reasonable, then stick to it.

The point of all this is: When you get to your writing, you will have only writing on your mind. Try it—you may be surprised.

SUGGESTIONS—CHAPTER 6

1. Make a priorities list. Consider family responsibilities, social life, volunteer work, chores, jobs, hobbies, schoolwork, sports, health, and cultural pursuits. Give each item on your list a number, with 1 being the highest priority. How high on the list is your writing? What would it take to move it up a notch?
2. Using your normal system of writing, keep a record of how many pages you have written at the end of each day, and by the end of the week. Then try the fifteen-minute-a-day method, keeping the same records. How do they compare?

BOOKS MENTIONED IN THIS CHAPTER
(IN ORDER OF APPEARANCE)

The Watsons Go to Birmingham—1963, Christopher Paul Curtis
Bud, Not Buddy, Christopher Paul Curtis

7

Learning Your Craft

How to Become a Better Writer

How can I develop an interesting style? How do I know what age reader I am writing for? Is my work any good if I have to keep revising it? Is there a way to have my manuscript looked at professionally before I send it to a publisher?

As you get deeper into the work of being a writer, these and many other questions will fill your head. Some will be answered as you continue to write, and as you read. Let the questions motivate you and guide you, not intimidate you. They show your natural curiosity and your need to find out more about this field that is still so new to you.

DEVELOPING STYLE

It is not unusual for first attempts at writing to be unclear, unformed, too dramatic, or not dramatic enough. Stories may be too light in substance to make into books. Trust that, as you write, your ability to use the written language and your ability to tell if a story has the proper depth and balance will grow, and your style will begin to emerge.

Style is not noticeable at first. Your very earliest attempts at writing probably show nothing but an eagerness to put words on paper, to communicate. Soon your personal way of seeing things will come through, and your particular facility with handling words and phrases, constructing sentences and paragraphs, will give your writing a mark of individuality.

Your style can improve as you go, but you cannot make it happen or watch it too closely. It is like watching your feet when you're learning to walk; if you watch to see how it's done, you stumble and fall. It has to happen naturally and easily. Once you are walking, however, there is nothing to stop you from adding a swagger, a hip swing, or a long stride to give your walk more individual character or flair.

AVOID CLUTTER

Concentrate on putting your ideas on paper. Make the writing as lively as you can, but keep your language simple and clear, avoiding devices like flashbacks and changes of viewpoint until you are more experienced. Avoid anything that will clutter your story.

You will probably have some idea about whether your book will be appropriate for very young children, half-grown children, or for teenagers, and that general idea is all that you need. You need not consciously write for a particular age group; believe it or not, your readers will find you. The age and behavior of the characters, the dialogue and settings you use, and the story line itself will suggest an age, even if it is not specified. Publishers impose an age on a book after it is written, mainly for cataloging and marketing purposes. "I need a book for a six-year-old," says a grandmother to a bookstore clerk who may or may not know all the books in the store by content. To help out the clerk, the publisher puts an easily broken age code on the flap of most children's books (your average nine-year-old can figure it out). The tag 0407 translates to ages 4 to 7; for example, 8/10; 3/5 means ages 8 to 10 or grades 3 to 5.

REVISION

All writers know that revision is inevitable, whether they like it or not. Some of us actually like the revision process. Rather than a chore, it seems to be another chance to look at our work, "re-see" it with new vision, and make adjustments to improve it. I have revised manuscripts five, ten, even twenty times to reach the point where I am satisfied.

Edit first for language. Look at verbs—are they active, and interesting? Do lots of word weeding; pull out the excess words and eliminate weak ones like "then," "and," "but," and "however," if you can. Avoid using them at the beginnings of sentences.

Edit next for style. Check the viewpoint; do a final plot check for soundness of structure and development; and read the dialogue out loud to "hear" if it sounds natural.

Finally, edit for efficiency. Aim for a tight, crisp text. Can you say what you have to say in fewer words? Then do it, for picture books, especially.

Your ability to revise and rework a manuscript shows your maturity as a writer. Your perceptions are constantly changing and reshaping; you may see something a third time around that totally escaped you before. Editors often see more clearly than the writer, who has a narrow vision of his work, and they can point out areas for improvement or strengthening. If you are rigid, unwilling to change words, sentences, paragraphs, and even characters, you may be sacrificing the success of the total book for the sake of a few well-crafted words. You, the writer, should be able to come up with equally wonderful words a second and even a third, fourth, and tenth time around.

FEEDBACK

Sometimes you need to come out of your writing cave to seek the help of others who have a sharper eye, who can see your work more critically than you can. Many writers depend on critique groups made up of fellow writers to give them important feedback on works-in-progress. These groups meet on a regular basis, and they can be made up of writers from a small geographic area who meet in the local library or their respective homes, or they can include members who never see one another but meet on-line at regular appointed times to share their work for that valued critique.

As you learn about your strengths and weaknesses, the trick is to work with the criticism you receive, and not against it. You may not always agree with what you hear, but do pay attention: you may find, above and beyond specific details, some larger truths that are important for you to consider. For example, if there is a question about the motivation of your main character, maybe your character is not drawn deeply or clearly enough. If there are constant problems with the story, perhaps there is a weakness in plot, or not enough conflict. Maybe it is a matter of clarity; if there is any confusion, examine the work for problems in language and structure.

For a professional evaluation, there are freelance editors who will consult with you privately and read and evaluate your manuscript for a fee (see appendix VII). Research these editors. Do they specialize in children's books? What are their credentials? Who are their successful clients? How long have they been in business? Agree in advance about the fee to be charged and be sure you understand what you can expect from the evaluation. A reading and overall report will generally cost less than a complex evaluation with specific line-by-line comments or follow-up readings after revision.

FURTHER STUDIES

For instruction in the writing craft, there are writing schools and courses of study that feature creative writing for writers of children's books, some of them by correspondence or online. These can be instrumental in helping you to understand the subtleties of plotting, characterization, form, and structure.

The Society of Children's Book Writers and Illustrators (SCBWI) has two annual conferences on the west and east coasts, and several regional ones, including some outside the United States. These conferences always feature well-established authors and illustrators and important people from the publishing world, and offer workshops in specialized areas such as picture books or writing historical fiction. At some, you can pay an additional fee to have one of the faculty critique your manuscript.

Numerous writers and illustrators offer private workshops and courses; the SCBWI may have a list of them, or search for them online to see what's available. Colleges and universities now offer graduate programs in, or with a concentration in, children's writing. These will demand much of you, in terms of both time and productivity, but if you are ready for serious study and development of your writing career, you might consider one of them (see appendix VII).

With this array of opportunities to study the field you love, there is no reason to struggle on your own for success. Eventually, you will be able to apply some self-evaluating questions to your work based on the criticism you hear from others. This is one certain way to avoid the serious mistake made by so many beginners—sending out material to agents and publishers before it is good enough, or ready, to publish.

SUGGESTIONS—CHAPTER 7

1. Find a children's writers' group in your area. Start in the most likely places—the local library or bookstore, writers' organizations, and magazines. If you cannot find one, how would you go about starting one?
2. Say you have a manuscript that you have taken as far as it can go, but you are not sure it is ready to submit to a publisher. How would you go about finding an editorial service? What criteria would you use for choosing one?
3. Find books on writing for children, and on writing in general, at your local bookstore or library, or online. Browse through them, if possible. Many of them will overlap in general information, but each book will offer different insights into the craft of writing. If you find a real favorite, it is worth buying it for your permanent reference collection.

PART THREE

Writing Your Book

What You Need to Know and Do

I think, I dream writing, and writing is who I am. How much time I spend at it, who I write for, why I wrote and what next I will write, fall in the realm of propaganda. The fact is that I must write and writing is work, hard and exacting.

> —VIRGINIA HAMILTON, from "Portrait of the Author as a Working Writer," *Elementary English*, April 1971

8

Writing Picture Books

The books that look the easiest to write—picture books—are, for many, the most difficult to write. Why? Because they depend on so few words to say so much.

A novel can have 50,000 words; a picture book may have fewer than 1,000. Those words must be well chosen. The renowned author Victor Hugo once wrote to a friend, "Sorry this letter is so long; I didn't have time to make it shorter." If you have ever written poetry, you can understand a bit better the difficulty of containing large thoughts in small spaces.

Careful crafting is necessary to tell a story in so few words. Yet economy is not enough. Not only must every word count, but the language of a picture book must be playful and fun; it should contain meaning and excitement; it should evoke memorable images and stretch the imagination and the child's understanding and use of language. This is a tall order, perhaps, but nothing less is acceptable.

KEEP THE STORY SIMPLE

Picture book stories deal with a single situation that involves some action on the part of the main character. You need not reach for exotic adventures to support a picture book plot. A situation that affects the child's everyday world has plenty of dramatic possibilities in it. You cannot find a less complicated yet more successful picture book than Ezra Jack Keats's *The Snowy*

Day, in which Peter is ecstatic to see that snow has fallen and goes out to play, and when he comes in, tries to keep a part of it by saving a snowball. The snowball melts and Peter is momentarily saddened by his loss, until the next day dawns and he sees new snow falling.

It is fine now and then to borrow a plot from an old folk tale, but this idea may, by now, have been overdone, in terms of the more familiar stories. There are already several versions of *Little Red Riding Hood* and *The Three Little Pigs* on the market. If you want to delve into the enormous stockpile of previously told tales, look into stories from other cultures that could use a good retelling for contemporary children. Or find a story that is slightly offbeat, although not too unusual to appeal to a large number of readers. When I chose to retell and illustrate *The Teeny Tiny Woman,* the only versions that existed were one in a storybook collection and one in a book that I felt did not do the story justice, because the book itself was tiny and therefore the simple delight of making everything appear teeny tiny in contrast to its surroundings was lacking. It was also not a story that was overly familiar to most children, although some adults remembered it as one of those tales told around a campfire when they were young. Therefore I felt justified introducing a version that I felt could meet the scrutiny of editors and book buyers.

THE CHILD'S-EYE VIEW

Focus on one main character and have all things happen from her point of view. Keep in mind the child's view of the world, rather than your adult view of things. Remember not only that a child stands much closer to the ground than an adult—maybe she is eye level with the family dog, or sees the knobs on the dresser while you see what's on top—but she also perceives from a child's viewpoint. How does the world look from behind her eyes? Capture the spontaneity and the child's wonder and sense of discovery; empower her to take action; have her come up with a solution to the plot problem. Be realistic; whatever she thinks, feels, or does must be appropriate to her age and her experience.

Not Necessarily Human

An animal or even a monster might represent the child heroine; she does not have to be human. Children see small creatures very much as they do other children. You will see, as you read more and more picture books, how animals are substituted for children. Remember Beatrix Potter's disobedient hero of *The Tale of Peter Rabbit* and H. A. Rey's *Curious George,* the mischievous monkey? And what about Russell Hoban's charming little badger in *Bedtime for Frances,* illustrated by Garth Williams? One almost forgets that the heroes of these stories are not human.

The Story Must Stand on Its Own

Many writers of picture-book texts rely, sometimes unconsciously, on illustrations to bring out their intentions, but the story should feel complete on its own. That does not mean you shouldn't think about the visual context. Of course you must remember to have something happen in the story for the artist to illustrate. To help you visualize, imagine your story as a film, and see how it moves, how the scenes change.

Text is almost always purchased separately from art. Unless the author is also the artist, illustrations are done by someone hired by the editor. If you are not an artist, you do not have to provide pictures, or find an illustrator, to submit your manuscript.

Most likely, when an editor accepts your story, it is because she likes it and there are good illustration possibilities, but also because there is some universal truth in it that she recognizes. Although the manuscript will be read and interpreted by the artist, who has her own vision, it is this universality of theme or behavior that will come through to the reader, not the specific visualization. A story you wrote with a kitten character in mind may well turn out to be a rabbit but your story will still work for the reader, as long as the animal chosen suits the behavior of the animal portrayed and the character you have drawn in your writing. (If you are an illustrator, see chapter 17.)

JUMP RIGHT IN

Your small reader will not wait for you to set up your background and describe your characters. If the story doesn't get off the ground right away, the child will simply pick up another book. Start your story immediately, with action. Grab the child's interest. Which of the following beginnings do you think works better?

Chadwick was a brown-and-white speckled dog.
or, Chadwick was lost.

I think you'll agree that the second one will perk up a lot more ears than the first. The vital word is *lost*; it trips our emotions and pulls us into the drama right away.

A picture-book text must be well-crafted so that a few words will create a small drama for the reader. Story action propels the book forward, so get right to it. Jump in. Take the plunge.

Include only details that will help move the story along; anything that the reader must know to understand the story. This is usually a lot less information than you think. It is not important that you tell the reader Jill has moved from her old house and is unhappy because she has no friends now and she is lonely. That will all come clear the minute Jill spots a little girl just about her age across the street, as she watches the moving men unload the truck. Keep the action going, pushing the story along to its peak and its conclusion, and never forget your aim.

BE HOPEFUL

Regardless of the subject, a book with a tone of hopelessness does not suit this age group. This does not mean that you should sugarcoat the facts, but you should be sensitive to the emotional capabilities of young children. No matter what has passed, hold out to the child a possibility for hope. Give her something to help her cope as she struggles with difficult concepts.

One of the finest writers for young people, Katherine Paterson, writes in her book *Gates of Excellence,* "I cannot, will not, withhold from my young readers the harsh realities of human hunger and suffering and loss, but neither will I neglect to plant that stubborn seed of hope that has enabled our race to outlast wars and famines and the destruction of death."

Where the Wild Things Are would not be the same book if Max had not found his dinner, still warm, waiting for him in his room when he returned from his visit to that place where the wild things cavort. In Judith Viorst's *Alexander and the Terrible, Horrible, No Good, Very Bad Day,* Alexander just can't get anything to go right, but his mother, at the end, assures him that some days are like that, "even in Australia." There is a certain justice and comfort in knowing that people at the far end of the world are having just as horrible a day, and Alexander is not alone. One feels that he will wake up in the morning open to the possibility of a better day ahead.

FIND THE PAGE-TURNING POINTS

Because of the concentrated form of picture books, there is a knack you must develop for moving the story along at appropriate "page-turning" points. A good rule of thumb is that there should be no more words on a page than are necessary for the time needed to look over the picture. Picture books progress much like short films, and, even if you are not an artist, you have to think visually to understand how they work. Just as the filmmaker keeps your interest by changing the scene continually, by varying the camera angles and the viewer's distance from the subject, and by the time spent on each scene, so you as the director of your story have to remember to add variety to your pages and to pace the work. You need to know when you have stayed too long in one spot or with the same characters, when to introduce action or humor, when to build suspense, when to peak, and when to decline. Look at Ron Roy's *Three Ducks Went Wandering,* with pictures by Paul Galdone, for a fine example of how page-turning points can work for a story. As the little ducks wander off, oblivious to the dangers that lie in wait, the reader is entertained by the clever use of mini-cliff-hangers.

The three ducks gobbled up the grasshoppers and then went wandering on through the woods, RIGHT IN FRONT OF . . . [page turn]

. . . A DEN OF HUNGRY FOXES!

Read Good Picture Books

Reading successful picture-book texts is one of the best ways to find out what makes one work. Listen to the language. Read books by Margaret Wise Brown, Vera Williams, Mem Fox, Ashley Bryan, and William Steig. Read the stories aloud and hear how the sounds trickle down to the ear. Be a child. Open up your imagination to what the words can do for you. In her book *Writing for Young Children,* Claudia Lewis reminds us "children are not to be thought of as any less receptive than adults to language that is art as well as communication. Primarily they want what we all want when we open a book—words that can work a little magic, a language strong enough to hold emotion."

Get a copy of *Where the Wild Things Are* by Maurice Sendak. Sit down with this book and study it. In it, you will see all that a children's picture book can and should be. Text and pictures work so harmoniously that when, for several pages, there are no words at all, the reader is hardly aware of their absence. Low-key colors and fine draftsmanship are far more appealing than eye-dazzling colors and shapes. The basis for the book is the psychologically sound story of Max, who is punished for being noisy and wild by being sent to his room. There he imagines that he sails off to a place where the wild things are, and he is in charge of them all. When he grows tired of the wild things, he sails home again to his little room, where he finds his dinner waiting for him, still warm.

Sendak designed the double-spread pages to lure the reader into their depths unaware—the drawings grow in size with each page until the exciting climax, when they cover the entire spread, then dwindle again, one by one as Max makes his way back to his room. You watch the trees grow out of the bedposts and push out of the frame of the picture as Max's imagination takes him away from the humdrum, restricted atmosphere of home to a place where all things are allowed and he is in command—every child's fantasy.

All of these factors are important to the total book and among the reasons for its success. There are some who say that the wild things scare little children, but for most children, the book is sheer delight, slightly dizzying with its implications of freedom and dangers never before experienced. The fact that everything comes right back home again where Max is safe and warm and someone cares seems to balance the exhilarating and dangerous adventure and keeps the wild things safely in their place. Isn't it also splendid that Sendak has them far away on a remote island and leaves them behind when Max returns home, implying that the wild things are not near enough to harm us? Isn't it clever that the worst thing the wild things do is make a lot of noise, gnash their terrible teeth, and roll their terrible eyes? There is nothing vicious about them, but children, with their structured lives and lively imaginations, probably see the chaos as scary.

Assume intelligence on the part of your reader. Don't be afraid to use big or interesting words if they seem right for your story. Words beyond the child's immediate understanding stretch her mind and her vocabulary. Letting the sounds roll around in her mind and on her tongue will help her learn how delightful the use of words to express ideas can be.

Look at the values represented in children's stories: love, friendship, courage, and honesty. Passing our values on to our children through stories is an old and respected tradition and will continue to survive. You don't have to preach to them, either. Just tell a good story. Children carry ideas with them, absorbed through their readings, long after the books have fallen apart.

THE VERY YOUNG READER

Books for very young children should be eye-catching. It is not strictly up to the illustrator to make them so. You must write with pictures in mind, even if you can't draw a stick figure. They must be ear-catching as well, so that children want to hear them again and again. The simple rhythms of nursery rhymes and repetitive tales, like *The Three Little Pigs,* or *The Little Red Hen* are delightful introductions to language. Simple stories and nonsense verse encourage playful words and sounds, and the actions of the characters suggest lively pictures. Simple word books to show concepts (counting, opposites, shapes, and so on) and to introduce letters and words are among a child's first books. Richard Scarry was a master of this genre; you may remember his books from your own early childhood. Books such as his *Early Words* contain labeled illustrations of all the items a child might see in his own surroundings, from a seesaw and a flower to a toothbrush and socks. Children begin to make the association of a word to a picture, a precursor to reading. The full-fledged story, generously imbued with humor and drama, comes a little later, as the child's attention span and experience grow.

A certain hit with the youngest readers is the cumulative tale, which has little plot but a lot of repetition. It continually builds, often to a hilarious and noisy climax. *The House That Jack Built* and *The Gingerbread Boy* are classic examples of these, but you can find recent books that use the repetitive format, like *The Napping House* by Audrey and Don Wood and *If You Give a Mouse a Cookie . . .* by Laura Joffe Numeroff.

Participation books are important because they involve the reader totally in the activity of reading through answering questions, acting out small dramas, discovering delightful details in the pictures, or coming up with solutions to problems. A good example of this kind of book is *The Jolly Postman or Other People's Letters,* by Allan and Janet Ahlberg which has letters, tucked inside envelopes, written by famous storybook characters to each other. Another is *Where's Spot?,* by Eric Hill, with many flaps to lift while the child tries to find the missing dog. Counting books like *One Dancing Drum* by Gail Kredenser are participation books, as they invite children to count numbers of musicians and their instruments as they arrive to play in the band.

A Few Taboos

There are no rules about what you should or should not write, but some themes are more in tune with current thinking than others. It can help a struggling new writer to understand some of the quirks in the patterns of children's book publishing. With few exceptions, stories about inanimate objects are seldom purchased because they are rarely successful. Some, such as Hardy Gramatky's *Little Toot,* have worked, but the writer is forced to exaggerate emotions to make the object more real, and the result can be too coy or whimsical. Sentimental stories about teardrops that talk and clouds with personalities do not stand up very well under the eyes of editors, who want more substance. Slim stories about desperately wanting something beyond reach *(A Pony for Jennifer)* or doing something extraordinary *(The Boy Who Could Fly)* have been done to death. Come up with a fresh approach if you are going to write picture books. Even though there are only a few basic plots upon which all literature is based, your way of seeing things, your unique artistic vision, should make your story fresh and exciting.

ANIMALS THAT TALK

There is a common belief that editors won't buy stories about animal characters that talk. This is not entirely true. James Cross Giblin, former editor of Clarion Books and award-winning author, speaking at a writers' conference about fantasy and the imagination, was asked, "Mr. Giblin, how do you feel about talking animals?" Giblin thought a moment and replied, "It depends on what they have to say." That's the truth of it. The fact is, if characters are drawn convincingly in a good, solid, well-crafted story, there is no problem. Look at the success of Rosemary Wells's stories about Max and Ruby (rabbits), or the Frances (badger) books by Russell Hoban, or Arnold Lobel's endearing characters in *Frog and Toad Are Friends,* and you'll see what I mean.

READ YOUR STORY ALOUD

When you have written your story, read it back out loud. Use a tape recorder if you have one so you can listen to it. Better yet, have a friend or a family member read your story to you. The author Sue Alexander found this procedure so valuable that, if her family members were not available, she would prevail upon passersby to come in to read her work out loud to her.

Listen to the story carefully. Have you given the characters life? Is there suspense? Is the dialogue believable? Were there dead spots where nothing happened and you could feel the pause? Did you grab the listener's attention and hold it? Have your words helped the story progress? Did you move your reader in some way? If you use the tape recorder, play the story three times in a row. Parents and people who work with children must read the same books over and over to small listeners, who delight in repetition. Your story must bear up under this severe test or some crazed parent will feed your book to the dog when the children are napping.

Make every word count. Imagine that you have to pay for each one published, say, twenty dollars. Can you save some money in that last paragraph? Five hundred dollars overall? A thousand?

CUT AND PASTE

A helpful exercise in understanding the flow of a picture book is to lay it out in thirty-two pages, the standard picture-book length. You don't have to be an artist for this. The layout is not for an editor to see, but for you to visualize your story and work out the flow of words and actions from page to page. (A professional dummy is discussed in chapter 17.)

Staple together sixteen sheets of plain white paper. Cut up a copy of your text and paste it in your thirty-two-page dummy book, breaking it up wherever you think it is appropriate to do so. Remember to allow room for the title page, the copyright notice, and the dedication, and any other front and back matter important to the book.

This all takes a good eye and ear and a superb sense of timing, so don't worry if you don't have it under your belt in one try. Seeing the dummy book with your words pasted in place will move you along more quickly to understanding the limitations of space that you must learn in writing picture books. Nowhere will you see more clearly the excesses in your writing or the problems in flow.

A good rule of thumb is to limit yourself to one action per double spread—or per page if the story falls into smaller, containable segments. Just keep in mind that, visually, the opposing pages should not fight each other in ideas or scope. This is the kind of thing that comes clear in the dummy that you may not see in a printed manuscript.

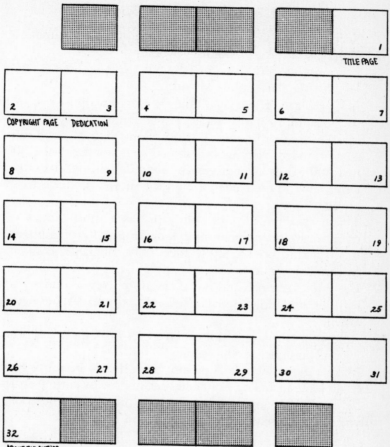

Layout for a thirty-two-page picture book. The first, second, last, and next-to-last shaded pages are pasted down to the book cover. If separate end papers are added to the book, all thirty-two pages can be used for text and illustration. Title page, copyright page, dedication, and other front and back matter deemed necessary to the book are taken out of these pages and must be figured in to the overall plan for the book.

CHECKLIST—PICTURE BOOKS

1. Keep the story simple and clear, based on a single situation.
2. Tell the story from a child's viewpoint.
3. Rely on your text alone to tell your story, without leaning on what the illustrations will do.
4. Jump right in. There is no time for long descriptions or rich background, so start your story action immediately.
5. Make every word count. Get rid of any that are not necessary. A modern picture book should be no longer than 1,000 to 1,500 words in length. Many are much shorter than that.
6. Offer hope to the reader, even if the subject matter is harsh or sad.
7. Think visually. Think of your story as a short film; keep things moving and interesting; look for page-turning points.
8. Read picture books. Study their style, language, content, rhythm, and values.
9. Use interesting rich and varied language. Never condescend by using simplistic language. Talk up to the reader, but never down.
10. Read your story out loud. Listen for its weak spots and how it bears up under several readings.
11. Make a dummy book. A picture book should be thirty-two pages long, including front and back matter. By cutting apart the text and arranging it page by page throughout the book, you will get a sense of pacing, flow, and balance.

SUGGESTIONS—CHAPTER 8

1. Read Ezra Jack Keats's *The Snowy Day*. Type the text out in manuscript format. Is it longer or shorter than you expected it to be? What have you learned about picture-book writing through this exercise?
2. Find a story you like in a folk tale collection that is no longer than 1,500 words, preferably shorter. Don't choose a picture-book version for this exercise. Make a photocopy of it and, using regular copy paper stapled together in a thirty-two-page folio, make a dummy book of the story. Cut up the text of the story and paste it in place as you think it would work best.

Books Mentioned in This Chapter
(in order of appearance)

The Snowy Day, Ezra Jack Keats
Little Red Riding Hood, many versions available
The Three Little Pigs, many versions available
The Teeny Tiny Woman, retold by Barbara Seuling
The Tale of Peter Rabbit, Beatrix Potter
Curious George, H. A. Rey
Bedtime for Frances, Russell Hoban
Gates of Excellence, Katherine Paterson
Where the Wild Things Are, Maurice Sendak
Alexander and the Terrible, Horrible, No Good, Very Bad Day,
    Judith Viorst
Three Ducks Went Wandering, Ron Roy
Writing for Young Children, Claudia Lewis
The Little Red Hen, found in many collections
Early Words, Richard Scarry
The House That Jack Built, many versions available
The Gingerbread Boy, many versions available
The Napping House, Audrey and Don Wood
If You Give a Mouse a Cookie . . . , Laura Joffe Numeroff
The Jolly Postman or Other People's Letters, Allan and
    Janet Ahlberg
Where's Spot?, Eric Hill
One Dancing Drum, Gail Kredenser
Little Toot, Hardy Gramatky
Max and Ruby (several titles), Rosemary Wells
Frog and Toad Are Friends, Arnold Lobel

And books by these authors:

Margaret Wise Brown
Vera Williams
Mem Fox
Ashley Bryan
William Steig
Sue Alexander

9

Writing Easy-to-Read Books

Have you ever looked closely at easy-to-read books? There is a pattern running through them. They are illustrated, but they are far from being picture books. Their appearance is usually similar to books for older children. The size and shape are not whimsical; this "older" look is a planned part of the package. A child who has learned to read feels that he is no longer a baby. No matter that he still secretly picks up his old picture books when nobody is looking, to enjoy once again the familiar pictures and love-worn pages; in front of his older brothers and sisters and his friends at school he is reading, and that puts him in the category of a "big boy." His books, then, must reflect this pride; they cannot look babyish.

Inside the book, you will find further concessions to the new reader: the large type is set fewer words to the line and fewer lines to the page than in a standard book, with a ragged (uneven) right margin to avoid a heavy block-of-type look. The space between the lines of type, or leading (rhymes with *wedding*), is generous. The text may be divided into sections or chapters; some books even have a table of contents. An easy reader like Dr. Seuss's *The Cat in the Hat* might have 1,500 words, but there are others with only 350 words, as in some of the Step into Reading books published by Random House, where there are various levels for emerging readers.

As a writer, it is good to keep in mind that easy readers have been wrought with care and conviction for this very important reader. The nuances of their success are worth examining.

AVOID THE TEXTBOOK SMELL

You may think that, since easy readers are for children who are just beginning to read on their own, they are made up of easy words chosen from a selected word list, but this is not true. Certainly there are books produced by educational publishers that do use the controlled vocabulary approach. For writers, they can pose a challenge that is like working the Sunday *New York Times* crossword puzzle—to take a list of allowable words and make a rollicking good story out of them. These books come from the educator's need to teach reading more effectively. Some of them are quite successful. Still, there is a difference between a teaching tool and a book created solely for the pleasure of reading. A child given a chance to read on his own will come to a book with a different attitude and expectations than one who is given a book designed to teach the development of skills.

The great success of most easy readers is that they do not use a controlled vocabulary and are genuinely compelling books with appealing design and interesting content. They are written by authors who understand that a good story is the important feature. Some of the words may never have been seen or mastered before, but readers will not mind that; they will eat them up, as long as the story has them in its grip. Children are young, but they are not stupid; they can smell a textbook a block away. It is no wonder they love easy readers, books that give them credit for their curiosity and intelligence. Perhaps this is one of the reasons we are seeing many schools using regular trade books in the classroom instead of textbooks.

If you feel that you want to write a book in the easy reader category, write it simply and forget word lists. The language should be rich and interesting. The sound and quality of the words and phrases are important. Otherwise you can end up with a see-Jane-run blandness. When you introduce a word that you think is a challenge for the reader, use it again later in the story. Once the child has mastered the word, it is useful for him to be able to repeat it several times until it becomes familiar.

Keep your sentences grammatically uncomplicated. Use simple, rather than complex, sentences, and avoid punctuation that elongates thoughts and ideas. Short, simple sentences are easier for the beginner to handle.

The plot must be simple, uncluttered, and developed along clear lines. The resolution, brought about by the hero or heroine of the story, must be satisfying to the reader. Sometimes, in easy readers, two characters may interact equally in the "hero" role, as in Arnold Lobel's *Frog and Toad Are Friends* in HarperCollins's I Can Read series. Generally, there is one clear main character in a story. (You will read more about that in chapter 11.)

Children love humor—funny characters and situations. Be lighthearted if your material permits. See the humor in your situations and your characters. Look at *Little Bear* by Else Holmelund Minarik, about the antics of a bear who could represent any six-year-old; or *The Know-Nothings* by Michele Spirn, about a group of well-meaning friends who bumble along amicably in spite of their total lack of skills in most areas.

Easy-to-read books may be easy to read, but they are not so easy to write. They take infinite patience, understanding of the beginning reader's abilities, and determination to get the story told in just the right balance of content and form. Arnold Lobel once said that the writing of the Frog and Toad stories was much more difficult than the illustrations; he worked harder with two sentences of text than with all the pictures in the book.

KEEP IT MOVING

Use dialogue whenever you can. Keep it short and snappy. The look of the text on the page is an important factor in easy readers. Lots of white space is a good thing, and dialogue helps to create white space: it gives life to the page as well as to the characters.

As in picture books, think in terms of moving your story along. Action is important; if your characters stand still too long, the reader gets restless. Have them do something interesting.

Try to describe your characters through their behavior and dialogue. Avoid extraneous detail.

Lillian Hoban, popular author and illustrator of *Silly Tilly's Thanksgiving Dinner*, among others, tried to include a single action in each sentence of her easy reader books. Bette Boegehold, author of the charming Pippa Mouse books, structured each sentence to contain an emotional idea. You get the picture. Pack it in, but keep it moving.

ENHANCE THE EXPERIENCE

Length varies in easy readers, depending on the reading level. Some are forty pages long but have fewer than two-thousand words. For more advanced beginning readers, the text could be denser.

As in picture books, watch out for wordiness. Make every word count. Break up the material into many paragraphs and divide your story into short chapters. Anything that lightens the act of reading visually will enhance the experience for a child who is still struggling to master a page filled with type.

CHECKLIST—EASY-TO-READ BOOKS

1. Write simply, but not with a word list in mind.
2. Use rich and interesting language; don't talk down to the reader.
3. Keep sentences short. Simple, rather than complex, sentences are best.
4. Repeat unfamiliar words to help the beginning reader.
5. Keep the plot simple.
6. Write with humor; children love to laugh.
7. Use dialogue often. It provides action and lots of white space on the page.
8. Create a single action in each sentence.
9. Avoid unnecessary detail that slows down the narrative.
10. Consider length; it can vary from 100 to 1,500 words, depending on the skill level of the new reader.

SUGGESTIONS—CHAPTER 9

1. Try to tell the story of *Jack and the Beanstalk* in easy-to-read form. Make a dummy book and pencil in the text or cut and paste it from a typed copy, as you envision it on the pages.
2. Look at easy-to-read books from different publishing houses. Compare them. Which do you think have the most effective formats?

BOOKS MENTIONED IN THIS CHAPTER
(IN ORDER OF APPEARANCE)

The Cat in the Hat, Dr. Seuss
Frog and Toad Are Friends, Arnold Lobel
Little Bear, Else Holmelund Minarik
The Know-Nothings, Michele Spirn
Silly Tilly's Thanksgiving Dinner, Lillian Hoban
Pippa Mouse, Bette Boegehold

And these series:

    Random House: Step into Reading
    HarperCollins: I Can Read

10

Writing Early Chapter Books

The term *chapter book* is technically correct for all books with chapters, but it has come to mean something special—another transitional stage—in children's books. Sometimes referred to as "early" chapter books, these books are the first real books, without special rules and formats, with which new readers engage. They look very much like any other middle-grade books.

Just as the easy-to-read book provides a transition for readers moving up from picture books to more complex stories that they can read on their own, early chapter books take young readers from about age seven to nine to another step along the way to independent reading.

MEATY STORIES

Readers in this age range who have mastered their basic reading skills want to tackle meatier stories, longer and more challenging than easy-to-read books, but may not yet be able to handle longer books with complicated plots. Subject matter can vary greatly, as long as it's something the reader cares about deeply. Relationships can be explored on many levels, and strong emotions are fine, but subtleties of plot are best kept to a minimum.

FEELING OF ACCOMPLISHMENT

Writers of early chapter books are no longer concerned with the difficulties of a child reading on her own for the first time. Words in type are now more familiar, and the denser page is not as intimidating as it once might have been, so there are fewer pictures. Many short chapters reinforce a sense of accomplishment as they enable the child to read a whole chapter in one sitting.

SINGLE IDEA

Structurally, plots remain simple and uncluttered. There is a small cast of characters, and all the action takes place within a short time span—a day or two, perhaps a week, or even a month. A story generally revolves around a single idea or situation, and the story builds around that idea with plenty of action and drama, with occasional simple subplots adding depth.

In my book, *Oh No, It's Robert,* for example, the main plot is about Robert struggling to win a classroom contest (the main plot) and while he is working at this, books from the classroom library are being scribbled in by someone whose identity he is determined to uncover (the subplot). One is closely related to the other, and there is nothing too subtle or too complicated about either.

MEASURING THE WORLD

In spite of their short chapters and overall small word count, these books do not shy away from intense relationships or strong emotions, although there is not as much character development or description as in longer books. Readers expect lots of action and dialogue.

Everyday experiences fill a seven- or eight-year-old child's world, and family is the familiar structure against which the outside world is measured. Adults still play a major role in the scheme of things—parents, teachers, neighbors, grandparents, and babysitters. You will find examples of this in my Robert books as well as in Cynthia Rylant's *Missing May,* Johanna Hurwitz's *Busybody Nora,* and in Megan McDonald's *Judy Moody.*

The above advice notwithstanding, all that applies to writing middle-grade novels applies here. Your characterization must be believable. Your story structure must be sound. Your dialogue must be smooth and natural. Read ahead to chapter 11 to get a capsule summary of what writing middle-grade novels involves, and then adapt from that to suit the early chapter book. You will find that there is little difference in the basic structure and form, although the early chapter book will abbreviate certain areas to accommodate the weight of the material against the age and reading experience of the child.

CHECKLIST—EARLY CHAPTER BOOKS

1. Stories are meatier, a step up from easy readers, but not yet as complex as middle-grade fiction.
2. Text is divided into many short chapters, so the reader can feel accomplishment with each chapter read.
3. Everyday experiences are often the basis for stories.
4. Adults still play a significant role in the life of heroes and heroines.
5. A single dramatic idea is sufficient although there could be a subplot.
6. Strong emotions or relationships are fine.
7. The early chapter book may look like an ordinary middle-grade book, but because of the larger type and leading, the length is generally shorter, in the 10,000- to 20,000-word range.

SUGGESTIONS—CHAPTER 10

1. Read several early chapter books. What is the idea on which each book is based? Who are the characters? Think of a situation on which you might base a story for seven- to ten-year-olds.
2. Choose one of the books you read in step 1. Write out a one-sentence summary of each chapter. This will help you see clearly how a chapter book is plotted and developed.

BOOKS MENTIONED IN THIS CHAPTER
(IN ORDER OF APPEARANCE)

Oh, No, It's Robert, Barbara Seuling
Missing May, Cynthia Rylant
Busybody Nora, Johanna Hurwitz
Judy Moody, Megan McDonald

11

Writing Fiction

Writing a novel is an intimate, exasperating, exhilarating, perplexing, immensely satisfying experience, with something new to learn at every turn. At the heart of it is a good story, but then there is more. How do you tell the story? Through which character's eyes? Against what background? How do you keep your reader with you, turning pages to find out what happens next? How do you juggle humor and suspense, believable incidents and dramatic scenes, and still have a clear plot with all its necessary layers and subplots?

There are more subtleties in writing a novel than this book can cover, but looking at some of the most basic elements, you will at least have an understanding of the form, and avoid many problems that can plague the beginner.

PLOT

E. M. Forster demonstrated the difference between story and plot this way:

The king died and the queen died. That's a simple story.

The king died and the queen died of grief. That's a plot. It shows not only what happened, but the effect of what happened.

Simplified, a plot is a plan of action; the steps taken by your protagonist to resolve a predicament or problem that bothers him, and the result of those actions. It is not just this happpened . . . and that happened . . . and then that happened. It involves more than mere curiosity about what happens next; the reader wants to know why things happen, and what effect actions of the story's characters have on the story's outcome.

The plot should be crystal clear in your mind or you will end up trying to plug holes and fix leaks that become increasingly difficult the more patching you do. A story can move along and characters can be amusing or lifelike without a plot. I know. I've done it. You get very nice comments from editors about the funny dialogue and the appealing characters, and in spite of all that, the manuscript is turned down time after time because the editor didn't know what it was about.

Twenty-Five Words or Less

If you start off with a vague plot idea it can go awry; you can lose focus and take too many unmanageable turns. One way to stay on track is to write out a one sentence summary—in twenty-five words or less—telling what the book is about. This is a tough exercise. Don't be alarmed if you find this difficult; most people do at first. It's a surefire way of finding out if your plot works or not; if you can't do it, your plot is in trouble.

Remember that your plot summary shows how your story moves from point A to point B and to point C, in a bare bones overview. The plot answers the question: "What is your book about?"

Subject Matter

Readers in the middle grades, from ages eight to twelve, like clearly defined plots with lots of suspense, humor, and action, but subject matter covers a wide range. Family stories, such as Laura Ingalls Wilder's Little House series and Sydney Taylor's *All-of-a-Kind Family* are worlds apart in culture and time, but the warm and loving family life makes them extremely popular with this age group.

Humor is enormously important. In *Joey Pigza Swallowed the Key* and its sequels, Jack Gantos demonstrates the kind of humor this audience loves, wrapped in a story about a real issue kids face on a daily basis in school—the hyperactive, disruptive kid.

Some kids love fantasy, from the traditional magical kind like *Harry Potter and the Sorcerer's Stone* by J. K. Rowling and *The Golden Compass* by Phillip Pullman, to futuristic stories, like M. T. Anderson's *Feed* or Lois Lowry's *The Giver*.

Mysteries, friendship and school stories, and stories about issues that were considered off limits just a few years ago, are all appealing to this age group. Today, readers in the middle grades and especially teenagers are reading about the world as it is, and that includes some difficult topics, like child abandonment, incest, mental illness, gangs, and violence.

Teenagers can handle complex plotting and strong issues. They are reading adult works as well as books designed for them, with teenage characters and concerns. They are ready to deal with ideas, probing beneath the surface of things. They want humor, too, but at this age it's a wackier sort. Stories often deal with personal relationships and the shaping of ideals.

Write about What You Know

You've heard the old saying, "Write about what you know." Reaching for exotic people and places for your stories may symbolize the freedom of a writer in that you may choose any subject, and let your mind wander freely. This sometimes works for the seasoned writer, but the reality is that it is quite a handful to take on an unfamiliar world and make it convincing to the reader. The result could be characters who move like cardboard cutouts, locations as fake as movie sets, and plots that are farfetched or confusing. When you are starting out, take hold of things and people you know and feelings you have experienced; they are what you know best, and you can make them come alive through your personal knowledge of them. Maybe your childhood was not glamorous or exciting, but you can still feel the cold coming through the hole in your mitten as you walked to school on a chilly winter morning, and you can almost taste the home-baked chocolate chip cookies your mom put in your lunch box. You can recall the fluttery stomach you had on the day you had to stand in front of the class and recite a poem. You remember the chilling loneliness when nobody was there to hear you and the imaginary people and places you invented to keep you company. This is what you should write about. If you want to set your story in another time, do your research on outer details, but transfer what you know from your own experiences to the characters in your story.

No Corny Gimmicks

Be sure that the problem your protagonist is confronted with will interest your readers. Work to make your plot convincing; don't use corny gimmicks and obvious devices to get yourself into and out of interesting situations. It is better to have ordinary events done in a believable way than to stretch your credibility in an effort to be clever.

CHARACTERS

As a beginner, try to have no more than four characters of any significance in your novel. Too many characters without real purpose can cause confusion and spread your reader's interest too thin, so keep the number to a minimum. Another rule of thumb is to give names only to the most important characters so the others remain in the background.

Your main character must be the one to solve the problem, or your story will fall flat. Nobody wants to stick with a person all through a story, sympathize with him, suffer with him, and then have someone else waltz away with the credit for tying up the problems of the book.

You can come up with full, rich, flesh-and-blood characters if you know them well enough. To do that, keep a character profile on each person who will appear in your story. Include his name; family background; school history; medical history; relatives and friends; his favorite color, TV program, and hobby. What was his favorite toy when he was little? How does he feel about math? Girls? School? What does he do in his spare time? Does he have any secrets, even from his best friend? What makes him blush, or go into a rage? Your secondary characters, as well as your protagonist, need profiles, but perhaps in less detail. These studies should enable you to show characters accurately in any situation. Show us their faults as well as their virtues, but draw us to your main character with a balance in favor of his virtue.

Motivation

The protagonist's motivation, his reasons for wanting to solve the particular problem of the plot, should be clear. If he doesn't want or need the solution badly enough, the reader will not be convinced by his actions. Let the reader know what's at stake if he fails. Show the reader what makes your characters tick; why they do what they do, so he can identify with their hopes, successes, and feelings.

SUBPLOTS

Stories for readers in the middle grades and older almost always have at least one subplot. These are separate story lines that run parallel to and help to advance the main plot. Toward the end of the book, they come together the way several streams will flow into a river. There is no rule about how many there should be; it depends on the depth you want your story to have, and your ability to handle them. Beginners find this aspect of plotting confusing, like learning to juggle. It is a skill that can be learned by most, and improved upon with practice.

For example, in the story *Harriet the Spy,* by Louise Fitzhugh, the main plot is about Harriet's classmates finding her spy notebook and seeing what she has said about them, but an important subplot is the loss of Ole Golly, Harriet's nanny, who has been a source of love, security, and guidance for Harriet's entire life.

BACKGROUND

Just as you round out your characters, you will have to create an authentic background for your book. The background tells us what we need to know about your characters and the situation presented to us as we begin to read. It can reflect the style and family history of your characters; it can be the church or religion that is mentioned here and there; it can be the street and the house and the room and the way the furniture is arranged in that room. It is how people talk, which reflects not only their geographic location but their education and their attitudes. Sometimes you will have to do a great deal of research to be accurate; if you write about a Danish girl in the period when Hitler was in power, as Lois Lowry did in *Number the Stars*, you'd better learn what it was like to be a Dane living in Denmark during the German occupation. If your story is about survival in the wild, as is Harry Mazer's *The Wild Kid*, or Jean Craighead George's *Julie of the Wolves*, you'd better learn something about living outdoors and survival techniques.

Even when you write fantasy, you must do it convincingly, by grounding it in the familiar. Sometimes, as in folk and fairy tales, a few well-chosen words like "Once upon a time" or "Long ago and far away" swiftly transport you from the real world into the make-believe. For futuristic novels, you must find ways to take your reader into the fantasy world and keep his belief suspended for the whole time that you are there. To do this, you will find that using commonplace details of life as we know it in our current time and place, and transfiguring them into comparable details in a future century, works wonders. Today, we speak; tomorrow, we may transmit thoughts electronically, but the common denominator is that we are "talking" to one another.

BEGINNING AND ENDING

As an editor, I found that many new writers actually began their stories on the first page of their second chapter. As a writer, I found how easily one could fall into this habit. With the physical descriptions of characters and places left behind in chapter 1, writers seem to feel free to move ahead with their story, and that is when the interesting part begins.

Look at your manuscript. When does it begin to grab the reader's interest? Examine the first lines of several children's novels and see how different authors start their books. Rarely will you find descriptions of characters or settings. This kind of basic information is woven into the text as the story progresses; it is wasteful to spend a whole chapter or a section of a chapter on it.

It should be clear from the outset what problem the protagonist must solve and, before too long, what he must do to make things right. That means immediately identifying your main character and the situation that makes him take action, before you do any explaining or setting of scenes, although some background might come through as you do this.

Now look at your ending—have you gone on too long? This is like the previous problem, but at the end of the book rather than at the beginning. Feeling the need to wrap things up and explain yourself, you may have gone on past the natural ending. Find the point at which the plot problem has been solved. If you have not made your intentions clear by now, a final wrap-up is not the solution, and it will be obvious—and boring—to the reader. Scrutinize your last paragraph, page, and chapter. Are they really necessary?

THEME

People are sometimes driven by their own strong personal values to tell stories, hoping to use fiction as a way to reach people. The idea is that while the reader is being entertained, he can also be warned, persuaded, or educated. Rarely does a moralistic story break through into popular acceptance, unless the author has enough talent to pull the materials away from the didactic approach and make it something more than a sermon. "Message" books are difficult to do successfully (with the message hidden enough to be palatable). Every book has its theme, of course, but that is a different matter.

That doesn't mean you won't be drawn to writing about issues that are important to you. The theme is the writer's topic, and his personal point of view on that topic is bound to come through. It is different from plot, which is what happens in your story.

If you feel strongly about guns, for example, and set out to write a book that will show a child how playing with a gun can lead to dire consequences, you will be preaching a sermon. Tell a good story that has your reader interested and involved in the main character who gets caught up in the conflict of what it is like when he is given a gun by a fellow gang member and suddenly gains a new level of respect from his enemies. See how Walter Dean Myers does just this—brilliantly—in the Newbery honor book *Scorpions*.

To understand clearly the difference between plot and theme, think of L. Frank Baum's *The Wonderful Wizard of Oz*. The theme is "Be it ever so humble, there's no place like home." The plot, on the other hand, is how Dorothy gets herself out of trouble and home again after a tornado drops her in the fantastical world of Oz.

Choose a theme that is appropriate for the age of the reader. Teenagers are struggling with ideals and values, and for this reason themes on moral courage frequently appear in the books they read, even when the books are romances exploring coming of age, alienation, and sexuality. Stories in today's novels deal with perceptive changes in a young person's life and insights into how kids cope with an overwhelming need for justice, principles, or compassion in a less than perfect world.

ACTION

Young readers of all ages want plenty of action in their books, not necessarily the cops-and-robbers or car-chase variety, but movement, involvement, a sense of something happening. More sophisticated readers can coast along for a while on crisp dialogue and stimulating ideas, on intricacies of plot and character development, but even with the advanced reader, you can't keep things quiet for too long. The reader wants to be engaged in the story action, to feel things are moving ahead, with a promise of interesting things to come.

Sometimes the lack of action, or the feeling that there is no action, can be traced to a problem that seems to grab hold of beginning writers. It is the compulsion to tell the reader what's happening, instead of showing him. Editors sometimes scribble "SDT" in the margins of manuscripts, standing for "show, don't tell," which indicates just how common a problem it is.

With apologies to Charles Perrault, here is an example—in my words—of a scene from *Cinderella* to illustrate the difference between telling and showing.

Telling

At the stroke of midnight, Cinderella left the Prince and ran from the ballroom, down the stairs to the coach below. One of her slippers fell off but there was no time to pick it up. She got in and the coach took off, arriving home just as the last chime of the clock rang, and everything turned back to the way it was before.

Showing

Bong.

Midnight! Where had the time gone?

"I must go," said Cinderella, breaking away from the Prince.

"Wait! Stop!" cried the Prince, running after her.

Cinderella turned to look.

Bong.

She picked up her skirts and dashed down the steps. In her hurry one of the glass slippers fell off. There was no time to stop and pick it up.

Bong.

The coach was waiting. She jumped in quickly.

"Hurry!" she cried.

The whip cracked and the horses flew through the night. Inside the coach, rocking and bumping along, Cinderella held her breath. Would she make it in time?

At the last stroke of midnight, almost home, they stopped. The horses and footmen were gone, and the coach had turned back into a pumpkin. Cinderella looked down. She was no longer in the beautiful ball gown but wearing again her familiar rags.

VIEWPOINT

Viewpoint is more than determining whether to tell your story in the first person or the third. It is getting inside the skin of the one character—usually the main character—and writing the story through that character's thoughts and feelings. You, as the writer, become the main character, in a sense, and think and feel as he does.

That means you cannot know what other characters think or know, unless they tell you, through dialogue or other means. You can only show what the main character can see, hear, or know about something. If the viewpoint shifts from character to character, it jerks the reader around, making it impossible or improbable to keep her attentive.

The advantage to having a single viewpoint character is that your reader will be able to get close to him, understand him, and share emotionally in his efforts. Therefore, the reader has to know what motivates him, how he thinks and feels. If you draw your protagonist well, and keep his viewpoint undiluted by the viewpoints of others, the reader should be able to identify with the character.

Describing the viewpoint character requires some stylistic gymnastics. Because you can't be in his skin and look at him at the same time, you have to think of ways to give certain physical information to your reader. One way is to have it come from someone else. A dialogue might include something like this:

"Chris, how come your hair is blond and curly and mine is straight and mousy brown? We're sisters, after all, and have the same parents."

You can also have it arise in the character's own thoughts or reflections:

Mark looked at the photo on his mom's dresser. People had told him he looked just like his father, but he had never thought about it before. They both had brown hair, it's true. And his eyes were blue, like his father's, but not as sad. Maybe it was his smile, that same crooked smile he had seen so many times in the photo album.

Once you have established your viewpoint character, you can think about how you will tell the story—in the first person or third person. A viewpoint should not be chosen because it is fashionable, but because it works for the kind of book you want to write. Each type of narration has advantages and disadvantages.

With the first person, you have to speak exactly as your character would; you can hardly avoid a heavy use of idiom if you want him to sound believable and natural. You never get away from the narrator's position, and see events only through his unique vision. For example: "I was a perfectly normal guy, just doing my locker thing, when Brenda entered my life. . . ." You have little perspective on the situation. Responses have to be from within the skin of your hero.

In third person, you are still in the protagonist's viewpoint, but are removed from that intensely personal position. For example: "Sam had just tossed his gym shorts into his locker and grabbed his biology book for third period when the most popular girl in school walked up to him. . . ." You step out of the narrator's shoes but you still stick close to him. In other words, you are not in his skin anymore, but you still see everything from his single view.

DESCRIPTION

For younger children, actions speak much more effectively than description. Look at Beverly Cleary's *Ribsy*, about Henry Huggins's dog. Ribsy is a living, breathing, slurping dog, and yet he is barely described. We know him by watching him sniff garbage, bark at a fish, and follow Henry around, wagging his tail exuberantly.

Details in books for older readers tend to help create atmosphere, but if they are implanted correctly, they do not intrude on the reader. Descriptive information about characters and settings should be woven into the action, and only if it gives the reader important details. In the opening of chapter 3 of Louis Sachar's *There's a Boy in the Girls' Bathroom*, we meet Bradley Chalkers's mom.

Bradley opened the front door to his house, then made a face. It smelled like fish.

"You're home early," his mother said from the kitchen. She was a large woman with fat arms. She was wearing a sleeveless green dress and holding a butcher knife.

"My friends and me, we raced home," he told her.

A fat fish, about the size of one of Mrs. Chalkers' arms, lay on a board on the counter. Bradley watched her raise the knife above the fish, then quickly hack off its head.

This passage gives the reader a better picture of Bradley's mom than a page of description could.

CONFLICT

There is no real story unless there is some obstacle to overcome. If Cinderella had no conditions to meet on the night of the ball, everyone would have danced happily ever after, but there would be no story in it. Conflict adds another layer to your story that gives it more substance, a challenge to show what your hero can do when up against the odds.

Decisions and problem-solving come with the job of novel writing; they are not easy and should not be presented as easy to your reader; having your hero struggle through some rough choices gives your protagonist more substance.

Joe wanted a catcher's mitt and got one.

There's no story there. However . . .

Joe was tired of being teased by the other boys, just because he didn't have his own catcher's mitt. He'd show them. The game was Saturday. He had to do something fast, but what? Would it be stealing if he just borrowed a mitt? He knew if he went to Kapper's after school he could hide one under his jacket and never be caught. Mr. Kapper was almost always too busy to notice him.

Aha. Now there's a story beginning to form, possibly with multiple layers, depending on Joe's choices and what happens.

In a well-balanced story, there is generally an inner conflict and an outer one. Again using Baum's *The Wonderful Wizard of Oz* as an example, surviving the cunning of the Wicked Witch of the West is Dorothy's outer conflict, while at the same time, she has to learn that her home and family mean everything to her—the inner conflict.

WATCH YOUR LANGUAGE

Dialogue should have a point. When your characters speak, what they say and how they say it should show us personality or background. Dialogue can also help to move your story along.

Janet McDonald's characters in *Twist and Turn* are inner-city kids living in the projects, and you know this as soon as they open their mouths. Ann M. Martin's girls in *The Baby-Sitters Club,* on the other hand, speak like adolescent girls all over the country who live in modest suburban homes, get an allowance, and follow the rules imposed by their parents and schools.

You will have to develop an ear for speech that can be absorbed, distilled, and put on paper without losing the quality that makes it real. Listen to the way young people speak to you, to their parents and teachers, and to each other; those are three different things. Listen to girls speaking to girls, girls speaking to boys, boys speaking to boys. Of course, this makes an eavesdropper out of you, but it's for a good cause. You want characters who speak as real people do, in a manner appropriate for the age, the speakers, and the place.

What makes accurate dialogue is not speech as it would be recorded on tape, but speech that helps to define your characters and sounds like the people you write about. Why are the two not the same? A novel shot through with dialogue such as this would be difficult to read on a sustained basis.

"Jeet?"
"No, joo?"
"Where ya goin'?"
"Jill's. Wanna come?"
"Nah."
"'Kay. 'Bye."
"See ya."

It would soon be boring, as well as difficult to follow. "Gotta," "dunno," "see ya," and other actual sounds made by young people in their shortcut speech look and sound wrong when set in print. Besides, it's sloppy characterization. You want to show the reader what the character sounds like, but it's up to you to figure out how to capture the spirit and feeling of speech without losing that spontaneous quality. Experiment. Try listening to young people engaged in conversation in various situations. Listen for how they speak as well as what they say. Are the sentences choppy? When they describe something that happened to them, what do they do to grab the listener's interest? Find out how authors who write in different styles handle dialogue. No two have done it the same way, and yet they are all are successful at it.

TAGS

Use the word *said* in dialogue, rather than a substitute like *growled* or *shouted,* unless you really want that tag to stand out. The word *said* is considered an invisible word, hardly noticeable to the reader and, therefore, invaluable because it does not get in the way of the action.

SUSPENSE

Telling the reader everything up front is a sure way to kill suspense. Any story needs "hooks" that keep pulling the reader along, offering him just enough to keep him satisfied but in the grip of the story. You don't want him to figure everything out before the story's climax and solution. That doesn't mean you must have cliff-hangers at the end of every chapter, but you do need to plant seeds of what is to come, and to foreshadow some of the important plot developments. For example, in a story that will lead up to someone falling from a high place, you might have a scene in an early chapter about someone dropping something, or something falling off a shelf and breaking, or in some way emphasizing the height of a flight of steps or a window. Even an elevator shaking before it reaches its floor, just enough to alarm the inhabitants momentarily, lays the groundwork for a later scene involving a real fall.

Don't Give Away Too Much

In a story called "Heather Gets Her Wish," you know everything turns out all right. There's nothing to worry about, and a good story makes you worry about something. Fiction titles may give you a notion of what the book is about, and maybe even tease a little, or allude to something symbolic, but should not give away vital information that will spoil it for the reader. *The Sisterhood of the Traveling Pants; When Zachary Beaver Came to Town; Bud, Not Buddy; The Ghost Belonged to Me; I Was a Teenage Fairy*—these titles all have a certain amount of intrigue about them and make us want to open the book to find out more. It is not always easy to come up with a good title, but it's worth the effort. Just don't give away too much.

Writing under a Series Name

This is a custom that goes way back. The popular Nancy Drew series was "written" by Carolyn Keene (who was actually its creator), Edward Statemeyer, and many different people who wrote—and still write—for the series over the years.

Writers who are hired to write for an existing series, such as the Baby-Sitters Club or the Saddle Club, generally get no credit, but if the creator of the series is generous, an acknowledgment on the copyright page may be made. They may be paid a flat fee and not receive a share of the royalties. Whatever the deal, it's good to establish it with full understanding at the time of signing a contract, because it's difficult to change afterward.

As long as you are aware of the pitfalls, there are wonderful opportunities for beginning writers in this genre. With some popular series producing a book a month, the demand for people who can write about previously developed characters, using plot lines created by others, is there. If you think you can write in the style of one of these series, send your resume and a writing sample to the publisher or packager, and ask if you might be considered as one of the writers for that particular series. You don't have to do this kind of job forever; it will not stifle your creativity. You will learn the ropes of the publishing world—how to work with an editor, how to revise a manuscript, how to schedule your work, how to produce work regularly and on time, and so forth. And, lo and behold, you get paid for writing!

A Strong Bond

There will always be controversy over what makes up "literature," and series may not fall easily into that category, although Laura Ingalls Wilder wrote an amazing series in her Little House books and no one has ever questioned their quality as fine books for children.

There's no doubt about it: children like reading about their favorite characters again and again, and doing so has provided a strong bond between readers and books for generations. Reading that provides pressure-free entertainment for fun in a world where children's lives are rigidly structured and academically driven by schools and parents, is as valid as any other. Even children need a little escapism now and then.

Length

A novel for the eight- to twelve-year-old generally runs from 30,000 to 40,000 words, or 120 to 160 manuscript pages. For readers twelve years old and up, manuscripts sometimes run longer, but not necessarily. There are young adult novels of 35,000 to 50,000 words, which means 140 to 200 manuscript pages. (I hasten to add that the Harry Potter series is a wild exception to the rules!)

Checklist—Novels

1. The plot is your plan of action. Sum it up in one sentence of twenty-five words or less. If you can't do this, your plot is probably in trouble.
2. Write about what you know. You will write more convincingly if you use your own experience as a guide.
3. Write a character profile on each important person in your story. These help you to create believable characters.
4. Your story's background must be authentic. You can invent it, but it must be grounded in what is familiar or real.

5. Be sure your beginning and ending are where they should be. Did you wait too long to start? Did you go on too long at the end?

6. The theme should be appropriate to the age and interests of your reader. Fiction is meant to entertain, not teach; avoid "message" stories.

7. Show, don't tell. Use action and dialogue to keep your story from being passive.

8. Have a single viewpoint. Write from one character's point of view.

9. Conflict introduces the element of choice and adds dimension to your story. Without it, you have no real story.

10. Dialogue should sound right for the characters, have a point, and help move the story along.

11. Suspense adds necessary tension. Don't give everything away immediately; hold something back to keep the reader interested.

12. Your title can help sell your book. Choose one with care, hinting at what the book is about but not giving too much away.

13. Watch your word count. For eight- to twelve-year-olds the average manuscript is around 30,000 to 40,000 words or 120 to 160 pages, while a manuscript for readers twelve and up can be anywhere from 35,000 to 50,000 words (or more) or 140 to 200 manuscript pages.

SUGGESTIONS—CHAPTER 11

1. How would you change the following to turn a simple story into a plot?

   Joey climbed into the snowmobile, started the engine, and went down the snowy hill.

2. Write a scene in which a nine-year-old child goes to the post office with a package to mail. Use authentic post office details to both establish the setting and reveal something of the child's personality.

BOOKS MENTIONED IN THIS CHAPTER
(IN ORDER OF APPEARANCE)

Little House series, Laura Ingalls Wilder
All-of-a-Kind Family, Sydney Taylor
Joey Pigza Swallowed the Key, Jack Gantos
Harry Potter and the Sorcerer's Stone (and sequels),
　　J. K. Rowling
The Golden Compass, Phillip Pullman
Feed, M. T. Anderson
The Giver, Lois Lowry
Harriet the Spy, Louise Fitzhugh
Number the Stars, Lois Lowry
The Wild Kid, Harry Mazer
Julie of the Wolves, Jean Craighead George
Scorpions, Walter Dean Myers
The Wonderful Wizard of Oz, L. Frank Baum
Cinderella, Charles Perrault
Ribsy, Beverly Cleary
There's a Boy in the Girls' Bathroom, Louis Sachar
Twist and Turn, Janet McDonald
The Baby-Sitters Club series, Ann M. Martin
The Sisterhood of the Traveling Pants, Ann Brashares
When Zachary Beaver Came to Town, Kimberly Willis Holt
Bud, Not Buddy, Christopher Paul Curtis
The Ghost Belonged to Me, Richard Peck
I Was a Teenage Fairy, Francesca Lia Block
Nancy Drew series, Carolyn Keene (pseudonmym for various
　　authors)
The Saddle Club series, Bonnie Bryant (and others)

12

Writing Nonfiction

If you have never thought about writing nonfiction, you might consider it; it is a good way to begin. It is one area in which your lack of credits will not stand in the way of the consideration of a good work on an appealing topic. Nonfiction writing for children can take many forms. It can be an explanation of how something works for young children, as in my book *Drip! Drop! How Water Gets to Your Tap,* in which Nancy Tobin, the artist, shows in detailed illustrations what I can only explain in a few words for an audience of four- to six-year-olds. It can be a well-researched and illustrated biography for middle-graders as in *Runaway Girl: The Artist Louise Bourgeois* by Jan Greenberg and Sandra Jordan. Or it can be a book of poems, as in Jesse Haas's *Horseprints: Horse Poems.* The variety in nonfiction subjects and style is enormous.

If you come up with a good idea and a fresh approach and show that you can handle it successfully through your proposal and sample material, your chances of "breaking in" could be significantly improved. For many beginners, expository writing is easier to handle than the complications of plot and characters, and once you have your outline in order, you cannot go too far astray, as you can with novels.

ZERO IN

The most important requirement of writing nonfiction is that you care about your subject. Choose a topic that really interests you, that you would enjoy learning about in some depth. Learn enough about that subject to write about it authoritatively. Then think of a way to explore some particular aspect of it, so that the subject is not too wide for your audience. Whales are exciting, but perhaps your book would have a better chance if you didn't try to cover everything there is to know about whales in general. Zero in on some portion of the larger topic of whales, such as the life cycle of a particular species of whale, or how whales communicate. Or let's say the Mayan culture fascinates you. There are many books already written on the Mayans, but you can make yours especially appealing by focusing on one aspect of Mayan culture, perhaps a study of their written language. A good example of this is Jim Murphy's *An American Plague: The True and Terrifying Story of the Yellow Fever Epidemic of 1793*. Here, Murphy takes a close look at a single event and makes an almost medical thriller out of it, as he brings a time and place to life.

No Need to Sugarcoat the Facts

Long ago, writers believed that they had to sweeten factual material for children, and created characters and stories to help the information go down. This is not the case anymore. Children love being entertained, but they also like clear straightforward information when they set out to explore a subject, especially in the early elementary grades. Marilyn Singer tells us, in *Prairie Dogs Kiss and Lobsters Wave: How Animals Say Hello,*

> A goose greeting a companion will stretch out its neck and hold it at an angle, curving it past its partner. At the same time, it will cackle. The more excited the goose is to see its mate or relative or friend, the more it will slant its head and neck and the louder and faster it will call.

Plain and simple, that's how geese say hello, just as promised in the title. No need to embellish; the facts are interesting enough in themselves.

Still, children have different tastes and moods, just as adults do. To understand the concept of the solar system, or just because it looks like fun to take a ride, a child may pick up *The Magic*

School Bus: Lost in the Solar System, one title in the popular series by Joanna Cole and Bruce Degen. Another child, doing a report for school, may choose Seymour Simon's book, *Our Solar System,* because the information is presented in a clear format of facts.

Older children appreciate a good anecdote or dramatization; this can enliven a subject and make it more personal. In Kathleen Krull's *Lives of the Writers,* she tells us that Louisa May Alcott's family lived "as poor as rats," and felt she was the only one who could raise them from poverty. She writes:

> Alcott locked herself in her room to write as many as fourteen hours a day. She worked neatly, pressing so hard with a steel pen that her right thumb became permanently paralyzed.

Krull cleverly chooses this bit of fact from her research to help show the writer's determination to succeed.

There is no question that actual incidents and individuals can perk up the text and reveal important insights. Take Ellen Levine's *Darkness over Denmark: The Danish Resistance and the Rescue of the Jews.* The author informs the reader of a time and place in history through the personal stories and remembrances of people who lived through it. She avoids invented dialogue and thoughts, which are fictional devices, and uses the voices of the people she interviewed to dramatize her material, along with actual letters, documents, and quotes.

The personal experience story is another means of conveying information through an actual person, yet keeping the nonfiction framework. Jill Krementz did this in *A Very Young Dancer,* in which the reader follows a young ballet student through her daily routine and on to a performance, showing the life of a dancer through the eyes of this one girl.

DISTILL THE INFORMATION

Once you choose and understand a subject about which you care deeply, distill and simplify the information to explain it in terms that the reader will understand. The amount of distillation depends on the age and experience of the reader. A few well-chosen details will be enough for an eight-year-old, for example, who wants a simple and direct explanation. For a teenager, you write at the interest and comprehension level of the average adult, which means that you can get into some pretty sophisticated concepts. Be careful with casual references to people or social and political events unfamiliar to your audience, without giving some information to the reader. Remember, the children who will be reading your book were born in the last fifteen years, and their idea of history is much different from yours. John F. Kennedy's assassination and the Vietnam War are history; the events of September 11 soon will be.

EXAMINE NONFICTION

Look at the nonfiction work of different writers. James C. Giblin writes about skyscrapers, chimney sweeps, and plagues, choosing subjects that appeal to his curiosity because he thoroughly enjoys the research. Stephen Swinburne, a naturalist and photographer, enjoys working outdoors with wildlife professionals as he did when he joined biologists at Yellowstone National Park where they were reintroducing grey wolves back to the area. His book, *Once a Wolf,* is about that experience. Russell Freedman is fascinated by great people in our past, and has written award-winning books on Abraham Lincoln, Eleanor Roosevelt, and the Wright Brothers. These authors' books are jam-packed with thoroughly fascinating information that is as entertaining as any work of fiction.

Roxane Orgill, in writing a young adult book about girl singers throughout the twentieth century, added fascinating sidebars about what they wore, and major forward advances in the music industry, without interrupting the flow and focus of her chapters, which were biographical, based on careers in music. These additional highlights gave the book a sense of time and place, and fit the musicians into the larger scope of what the world was like in particular decades.

In my book for younger readers, *From Head to Toe: The Amazing Story of Your Body and How It Works,* I lightened the look and feeling of the book by adding interesting tidbits about the body, which illustrator Ed Miller incorporated in his jazzy designs throughout the book. That kept the regular text in focus, while the side bars added liveliness and humor.

FACTS INTO FICTION

When does fact become fiction? Some writers take the facts and then build stories on them, inventing characters, dialogue, and thoughts. They are writing about history, but they're doing it as fiction. In planning to write a book about John James Audubon, Barbara Brenner found that a young assistant had accompanied the naturalist on some of his trips to sketch birds. Her imagination took over, and she told the story from the point of view of the boy, as if it actually happened, which she felt would be more appealing to young readers than a traditional biography of the naturalist. Thus *On the Trail With Mr. Audubon,* though factually correct, and a good portrait of the man, is considered historical fiction.

A GOOD TITLE

As in fiction, never underestimate the importance of a good title for your nonfiction book. Seymour Simon, well-known author of many fine books for young readers, titled one of his books *Chemistry in the Kitchen.* The book was reviewed well, but Vicki Cobb's book, similar to Simon's in content and published around the same time, was titled *Science Experiments You Can Eat* and became a runaway success. One can easily conclude that the funny, imaginative, eye-catching title of the Cobb book gave it the edge.

With my own books, I know from letters I receive that the zany titles of my Little-Known-Fact books, such as *You Can't Eat Peanuts in Church and Other Little-Known Laws,* and *The Man in the Moon Is Upside Down in Argentina and Other Little-Known Facts about Geography,* are often the reason why readers pick them up in the first place. There seems to be something about a breath-catching title that is funny and irresistable to some readers. Straightforward titles, however, perhaps with a self-explanatory subtitle, like *From Head to Toe: The Amazing Human Body and How It Works,* or *Fireboat: The Heroic Adventures of the John J. Harvey,* by Maira Kalman, are still found on the majority of nonfiction books, telling the reader exactly what to expect.

WHERE TO RESEARCH

Since successful nonfiction depends on the proper presentation of ideas and thorough research, I recommend that you carefully study chapter 15 on queries and proposals. Also look into research techniques and resources beyond the usual. Make it your business to find out what materials are available on your subject and then go after them. Be creative.

The Internet is certain to provide you with the information you need for a good beginning, but it may be only a beginning, depending on how much deeper you want to go into your subject. Consider the time you have available to do your research, and how much information you will need before you can cover your subject intelligently and come up with a workable plan.

With a bit of probing, you will find organizations or individuals with special connections to your subject, and people with some amount of expertise who might be willing to be interviewed or answer specific questions that have not been answered satisfactorily in books.

When you are dealing with facts, your sources must be impeccable. Responsible researchers verify their information by means of cross-checking with two or three reliable sources, or by having the top person or people in the field look at their manuscript. The Internet is fast and far-reaching, and has expanded the resources that we can tap into, but individual Web sites are not necessarily reliable or up to date, so you have to be careful about using them as your main source of information.

I remember calling the American Museum of Natural History in New York City to confirm my findings about the odd migration pattern of the monarch butterfly, which affected exactly one sentence in a book I was working on. I spoke to the chairman of the department of entomology, a charming gentleman who was delighted to talk to me about monarchs and proceeded to give me much more material than I could ever hope to use. He was all the more helpful when he understood that I was writing for children. Scholars, in their infinite wisdom, have considerable respect for passing on accurate information to young people.

KNOW WHEN TO STOP

There is so much fascinating information waiting for you that it will be hard to stop; you will probably over-research your book. That isn't a bad thing; you need at least three times as much material as you will use. It is important to have a big cushion of information from which to select. But if you have a deadline and the research keeps on going, you will simply have to call a halt to it and stop taking in new information.

If you have an editor interested in and waiting for a project you have proposed, and you find yourself deviating significantly from your outline because you have discovered new information you want to include in your book, let the editor know. Tell him about the new turn you have taken and estimate how long it will take you to complete the work.

KEEP GOOD RECORDS

The records you keep as you research should reflect all the important sources that you have used. You may need them later, for compiling a bibliography and for answering the letters you may receive from readers after the book is published.

Whenever you use other people's material, even pictures, you must give credit to the source, so take down all the information you can the first time you note it: book title, chapter, page number, library reference number, issue, volume, date, photographer, and anything else you may need in the future. Also note existing credit lines. These notes will save you the trouble of going back to these same sources later, which is time-consuming and sometimes even impossible.

If you want to use more than the fifty to two hundred words generally accepted as "fair use" from a written work that is protected by copyright, you will have to get permission to use them. Lines of poetry and song lyrics are viewed more protectively than most prose, so this rule of thumb will not apply. Your publisher may help you by giving its judgment on fair use or by providing the proper forms for you to fill out. Your contract spells out who is responsible for permission fees, should you need to purchase any of this material, so be sure to discuss this at the time you sign the contract.

The average length of a nonfiction book is roughly the same as for fiction, but much depends on the age of the reader and the type of material covered. For example, the picture book designed for older readers may be longer than the traditional picture book for toddlers. Photographs may play a large part in a middle-grade book, so perhaps the text will be comparatively shorter than a book of fiction for that same age group.

CHECKLIST—NONFICTION

1. Choose a subject you care about and would enjoy researching.
2. Don't sugarcoat facts; children are perfectly happy with factual information.
3. Distill and simplify to meet the needs of your audience.
4. Create a good title for your book.
5. Research your subject well and cross-check your information with two or three reliable sources. Go to the experts in the field.
6. Keep clear records so you don't have to go back to your sources later. These are helpful for permissions, answering editors' queries, preparing bibliographies, and so on.

SUGGESTIONS—CHAPTER 12

1. Choose a subject that you know you would like to explore. Do some basic research on it to see if it's as interesting as you thought it would be.
2. How many different ways can you think of to present your subject to the reader?

BOOKS MENTIONED IN THIS CHAPTER
(IN ORDER OF APPEARANCE)

Drip! Drop! How Water Gets to Your Tap, Barbara Seuling
Runaway Girl: The Artist Louise Bourgeois, Jan Greenberg and Sandra Jordan
Horseprints: Horse Poems, Jesse Haas

An American Plague: The True and Terrifying Story of the Yellow Fever Epidemic of 1793, Jim Murphy
Prairie Dogs Kiss and Lobsters Wave: How Animals Say Hello, Marilyn Singer
The Magic School Bus: Lost in the Solar System, Joanna Cole and Bruce Degen
Our Solar System, Seymour Simon
Lives of the Writers, Kathleen Krull
Darkness over Denmark: The Danish Resistance and the Rescue of the Jews, Ellen Levine
A Very Young Dancer, Jill Krementz
The Skyscrapers Book; Chimneysweeps: Yesterday and Today; When Plague Strikes: The Black Death, Smallpox, Aids, James Cross Giblin
Once a Wolf, Stephen Swinburne
Lincoln: A Photobiography, Russell Freedman
Eleanor Roosevelt: A Life of Discovery, Russell Freedman
The Wright Brothers: How They Invented the Airplane, Russell Freedman
From Head to Toe: The Amazing Human Body and How It Works, Barbara Seuling
On The Trail with Mr. Audubon, Barbara Brenner
Chemistry in the Kitchen, Seymour Simon
Science Experiments You Can Eat, Vicki Cobb
You Can't Eat Peanuts in Church and Other Little-Known Laws, Barbara Seuling
The Man in the Moon Is Upside Down in Argentina and Other Little-Known Facts about Geography, Barbara Seuling
Fireboat: The Heroic Adventures of the John J. Harvey, Maira Kalman

13

Writing in Verse

Poetry is enormously popular. Children love to read poetry, perhaps because of its short form: a few carefully chosen words are packed with ideas, emotion, and sometimes humor. Children learning to read find poetry comfortable because of its light look on the page and the repetition and rhyme in some poems that can help them to learn and figure out sounds and words for themselves.

Publishers continue to fill the demand for poetry with offerings ranging from collections by individual poets, like *Exploding Gravy: Poems to Make You Laugh*, by X. J. Kennedy or anthologies, such as those organized by theme and edited by poet Lee Bennett Hopkins, as in *Hoofbeats, Claws, and Rippled Fins: Creature Poems*. Many of our best picture books are written in verse. In 1997, Karen Hesse added a new dimension to writing in verse for children, when she published *Out of the Dust*, a novel in free verse. Not only did it win the Newbery Medal for its exquisite writing and elegant crafting; it opened a door for other writers who began to use verse more freely. *Locomotion*, by Jacqueline Woodson, is the poignant story of a boy recovering from the trauma of losing his family, through the poetry he writes for school assignments. Even biography has been touched by verse. In *Carver: A Life in Poems*, Marilyn Nelson gives us a revealing portrait of George Washington Carver through her poems.

STRONG ATTRACTION

You may have your own strong attraction to the verse form. Poetry looks so easy to write with its neat rows of words, spoken to a beat. Rhymes and chants of childhood nursery songs and games are probably still firmly implanted in your memory. Some of your favorite books as a child might have included those by Dr. Seuss, written in rhyme. If these books are so popular, and children relate to poetry easily and comfortably, then wouldn't it be neat to write your story in verse?

NOT AS EASY AS IT LOOKS

Poetry is a specialized form, and just like the perfect Native American clay pot or Japanese brush stroke, is deceptive in its apparent simplicity. The beginning writer, so new to writing and inexperienced in using written language to communicate ideas to children, may be drawn to it because it seems so free and easy, but, alas, it is not as easy as it looks. Writers of vast experience will tell you it is extremely difficult to write good verse at all; to write a complete story in verse is a challenge few take on successfully.

Editors find much of the material submitted to them is poorly written. Unskilled writers lean on the verse form to hide weak plots and poor characterization. Worse, they force rhymes and create singsong patterns—so obvious to the professional eye—that set the teeth on edge. It is no wonder that editors at some publishing houses discourage submissions in verse; reading through it takes valuable staff time from other writers.

READ GOOD POETRY

If you like writing in verse, get to know what good poetry looks and sounds like. Read plenty of poetry; there are wonderful collections and anthologies that offer an orderly and scholarly way to look at the work of one author or to hear many voices speaking on a single theme. Several are listed in the bibliography in appendix VIII.

If you write poetry in general, and have mastered the verse form, try to sell individual poems to children's magazines. It is a starting place to gain the much-needed credits you will need if you hope to publish a collection of your poems some day. Your reputation will grow over a period of time with the publication of your poems, one by one.

BE YOUR OWN CRITIC

Even if you have a natural ear for verse and have written it smoothly all your life, you probably have certain blind spots when it comes to writing a story in verse. Do you ever use an inferior word just for the sake of rhyming? Is your rhyme and rhythm singsong instead of easy and natural? Is your idea fresh and original, or has it been used many times before? Do you get caught up in the structure and form of the poetry and end up being wordier than you would in straight prose?

Remember that in writing a story, the principles of sound story form and structure always apply. Write about subjects, amusing and serious, that are familiar to children. Plot, characterization, and form must stand up to the same scrutiny in verse as they do in prose. In verse, an additional obstacle is that the slightest dip in maintaining a solid story structure can pitch the writer into the worst sea of doggerel.

A common mistake of beginners is getting too "cute" or sentimental with names or descriptions, or milking the emotions for effect, forgetting about story tension and depth of character. A sad little teardrop who wants to be a cloud has no more than a momentary pull on our attention; a child (or rabbit, or mouse) who shows courage by venturing into the unknown to save his brother is someone we want to know.

In verse, more than in any other kind of writing (even picture books), every word counts. Give life to your words by using language as a child does, with delight and wonder. Think of a child savoring new words that bubble, or bounce, or spill, and try to capture some of that in your words. Make the verse sing on the page, with shapes and sounds to satisfy the eye and ear as well as the mind.

REACH DEEP WITHIN YOU

Children are drawn to truth and vitality. Strong images are okay; you need not coddle the reader with sugarcoated silliness to get a point across. Reach deep within you for feelings, insights, and perceptions. Strive for rich, colorful images through carefully selected words, powerful rhythms, and a lively tempo. That is a tough order, but you cannot give young readers anything less.

Be hard on yourself as you compare your work to that of recognized and published writers. It will be no harsher than having an editor judge your work. If this stops you from writing poor verse, so much the better. If it inspires you to learn and to craft your words with a love of language, and you can make your poetry rise above the rest, that's what you're striving for, isn't it?

MAKE A CHOICE

In writing picture books, whether you do it in prose or poetry, do it so the writing and the rhythm is musical. Mem Fox writes sometimes in verse, sometimes in prose, but always with a lyrical cadence, as in *Possum Magic*. A gifted storyteller, she knows how to use words and patterns to tell a story for the best effect on the reader. Read her works aloud and you will hear the poetry.

Another writer whose lyrical prose contains powerful images is William Steig. Who can forget the mouse Amos, in William Steig's *Amos and Boris*, as he floats along on a piece of wrecked ship, under a starry sky, contemplating the universe.

> One night, in a phosphorescent sea, he marveled at the sight of some whales spouting luminous water; and later, lying on the deck of his boat gazing at the immense, starry sky, the tiny mouse Amos, a little speck of a living thing in the vast living universe, felt thoroughly akin to it all.

If you find that you fall into verse easily but cannot write prose without difficulty, chances are you need to work on your writing skills before attempting verse. Write your story in prose until it is clearly presented and satisfying. If you can do this with ease, yet the verse form still calls to you, then you can make a deliberate choice to write your story in verse. The form you use to write your story should always be a choice you make because it is appropriate to your material, not the easy way out.

CHECKLIST—POETRY

1. Read plenty of poetry; learn to recognize good poetry when you see it.
2. Apply the principles of good story writing when you write a story in verse.
3. Be truthful; reach deep within you for honest feelings, insights, and perceptions.
4. Use rich, colorful language and powerful imagery.
5. Learn to write well in prose as well as poetry; when you write in verse it should be a conscious decision to do so, not your only choice.

SUGGESTIONS—CHAPTER 13

1. Compare three picture books written in verse. Look at them stylistically, and for content and structure. What are the similarities? What are the differences? In each case, does it seem that this was the only form in which the story could work as effectively as it did? In what ways does the verse enhance the story?
2. Write a version of a familiar story in verse, for example, *Goldilocks and the Three Bears*. What are the strong points in your verse version? What are the weak spots? Why?

BOOKS MENTIONED IN THIS CHAPTER
(IN ORDER OF APPEARANCE)

Exploding Gravy: Poems to Make You Laugh, X. J. Kennedy
Hoofbeats, Claws, and Rippled Fins: Creature Poems,
    Lee Bennett Hopkins, editor
Out of the Dust, Karen Hesse
Locomotion, Jacqueline Woodson
Carver: A Life in Poems, Marilyn Nelson
Possum Magic, Mem Fox
Amos and Boris, William Steig

14

Writing Plays

A play may be unlike any other written work in form, yet the same rules of good storytelling apply. The two big differences are (1) in a play, the story is told entirely through action and dialogue, and (2) a play may be seen rather than read by much of your audience.

Writing plays is excellent groundwork for writing fiction of any kind, because it forces you to see in terms of movement, with action and dialogue pushing the story along. It is also terrific training if you plan some day to write for TV or the movies, both intensely competitive fields.

Sue Alexander, whose many books for children include picture books, says that writing plays can help you in your understanding of picture books and of the roles of the writer and illustrator. If you think of the book as a play, the writer is responsible for stage directions, dialogue, and actions, while the illustrator is responsible for props, settings, lighting, and costumes.

POPULAR SUBJECTS

Holidays, mysteries, humor, romance, home and school situations, and curriculum-oriented events remain the most popular subjects for original children's plays, and schools are where they are mostly performed. In addition, there are always adaptations of folk and fairy tales, bible stories, and biographies, often done in conjunction with the celebration of a holiday, like Christmas,

Halloween, or Martin Luther King's birthday. One biographical play that immediately comes to mind is *A Woman Called Truth,* a play about Sojourner Truth by award-winning playwrite, Sandra Fenichel Asher.

Dramatizations of popular books can make good plays, but before you take a story to make it into a play, you must get permission to do so from the publisher of the work, unless it is in the public domain, which means the copyright has expired and it is open to free use. If it is not, either choose another story, which is, by far, the easier route, or write to the publisher to request permission to make an adaptation. There may be a fee involved as well.

PLOT

The plot should be hinted at in the opening lines of your play. This primes the audience for the main character's appearance and the plot problem. The protagonist must be involved directly in the plot problem, and must solve (or help to solve) that problem by the end of the play.

The story must move forward continually, with tension building through complications, to dramatic high points that come in a series of waves. The highest peak, or climax, comes with one major wave, followed by the denouement, or resolution, of the plot problem.

BARE BONES

Writing your play may be easier to do if you start with an outline, getting the bare bones of it on paper. Figure out who your characters are, what will happen in each of your acts, or scenes, and how you will develop your story.

Traditionally, plays for young people are written and performed with one or two acts, and each act may be further divided into scenes. The main character should be introduced right away. If she cannot be on stage when the play opens, the dialogue of other characters should tell the audience about her, and let them know her importance in the scheme of things. The plot problem, which will involve the protagonist, should also be introduced in this first scene. This will set the mood for the whole play and give the audience important background to the situation. Just as you do in novels or chapter books, increase the story tension as the play moves along toward a high dramatic point, usually somewhere past the middle.

Your protagonist will eventually come to a crisis point at which time it should seem that things can't get any worse and the protagonist can't possibly get what she's after. This must worry the audience a bit before you provide the play's resolution in a believable manner. Then, you must show your protagonist getting past the obstacle through some clever or heroic means, and wrap up your story, all relatively quickly. Once the problem is solved, the story is over, so you have to answer all the unanswered questions and end the play. A surprise twist at the end is always "good theater."

As a newcomer to the art of play writing, consider the one-act play. For performing in the classroom, a play in a single act, and even with a single scene, is useful for teachers and students alike. It is easier to hold the interest of the performers and the audience with one continuous act than it is with a play broken up by one or two intermissions. For this reason, publishers buy more one-act plays for children than any other kind.

Beginning, Middle, and End

In a one-act play, divide it into beginning, middle, and end just as you would with any story. The beginning would establish the situation, the main character, and the plot problem. The development of the plot and the obstacles the protagonist faces fill the middle section, with tension increasing steadily. The ending includes the climax and resolution of the problem.

After the "bones" are laid out, you can begin to fill in the rest, because now you have a blueprint for the entire play and will know how to apportion your time, your characters, and your emotional content.

Characters

The number of characters in a play does not have to be limited, as in a novel, because the audience can see the different characters and tell them apart more easily than they can in print. You might need some specific identifying features to keep your characters separate and distinct from each other if they are close in age or appearance. One character might have a mannerism, like peering out over the rims of her glasses, or fluttering her hands when she talks, but it will wear thin if you try to have a different mannerism for each of your characters.

If there is an old lady who lives next door in your play, listing "OLD LADY" in your cast of characters may be enough. However, if it is important that your old lady be played as high-strung and nervous, you can add descriptive notes when she first appears, or has lines to speak. For example:

OLD LADY: [wringing her hands as she speaks] I wonder what could have happened to Mister Henderson.

This behavior gives the audience a clue to her character, while her physical appearance, except for the fact that she's old, is unimportant.

Do character studies for plays just as you would do for novels. Attention to characterization will help make your play live and breathe.

FLEXIBLE CAST

If your play is to be performed by children, and likely to be used in schools, it would help those putting on the play to have a flexible cast, so every child in the class can have a part—a band of pirates, a regiment of soldiers, or many townspeople—either all to be on stage at once or in shifts. However, in professional theaters, where the shows go on tour, small casts are preferred, where a few actors can play multiple roles.

DIALOGUE

The dialogue of a play accomplishes so much that it must be crafted with great care. You have to plant clues to reveal developments in the plot and the characters' motivations, and to tell what is happening offstage, yet you must be brisk and entertaining, to keep the audience's interest.

If it is a funny play, the audience must be given enough time to laugh so as not to cover over anything that might be said that is important to understanding the play. Too much laughter at a crucial point can throw off the rhythm and balance of the surrounding drama.

The young audience won't sit still for long speeches. Therefore, in dialogue and action, you must get across what is important in as few words as possible, cleverly composed for maximum effect.

ACTION

A play is not only words coming out of an actor's mouth, but movements as well. Although you are providing only the skeleton of the play with your script (the director, designers, and actors flesh it out), think in terms of stage movement as you create your play, just as you think about page turns in picture books, to help you to keep up the pace and not remain in the same place, mentally, for too long.

You don't have to tell actors how to move on stage, or worry about them bumping into each other. It's the director's job to block the moves so nobody trips over a table or chair or another actor as they move to deliver their lines. Your job is to mold the words to make the plot move along.

SETS

The playwright suggests only what is absolutely necessary to the plot, such as a table that must be positioned for certain actions to take place, or a lamp that is vital to the plot. Otherwise, set decoration is the set designer's job.

Plays to be performed by children and acted in schools and churches will probably have a small budget, and therefore should have limited sets. Keep this in mind as you write, so that your play does not require elaborate, out-of-reach equipment. Children—particularly those under age nine—love being in plays, and their minds are wide open to pretending. They don't need a fancy set: a single chair can be a car, or two chairs can be the bleachers at a football stadium.

Limit your production to one set. If you are changing scenes during your play, you may want to indicate changes more with the time of day or a cosmetic change in the decor (to indicate a change of styles as time passes) rather than with a change of location.

If something must happen in a different place, rather than create another set in which to do it, have your characters talk about what happens elsewhere, or have someone come in and tell other characters what she has just seen.

If you must have a change of scenes, and you're in a small space, such as a classroom, try having two children walk out on stage holding a sheet between them as a backdrop for the new scene. If the stage is large, and you have some lights, you might use "area staging," which means different areas of the stage—upstage center (farthest from the audience), downstage center (closest to the audience), stage right and stage left (from the viewpoint of the actor)—can be used for different scenes. Lighting can be managed so that the area on which the light is focused is the current scene while the others remain in darkness.

COSTUMES

Setting a play in another time is difficult because costumes may be necessary or at least desirable to help set the historical period. Costumes should be as simple as possible: a hat made of construction paper or a sash to represent a soldier's uniform.

"Don't ask kids to do or find things that are impossible," says Sue Alexander, who has written many plays for children. She recalled reading a play that required thirty Confederate Army uniforms! Alexander says children may come up with a substitute for the uniforms, such as thirty gray sashes, but they will think they are not doing it right.

PROPS

Props, or properties, needed for a play should also be things accessible to children, such as brooms, pillows, and pitchers, or you should suggest how they can find them. Items such as swords can be made with some help from parents or teachers, but keep in mind that not everyone has the time or ability to make a papier-mâché donkey, for example.

A single item can represent a whole atmosphere, if it is chosen correctly. A piece of cardboard with a sheet of aluminum foil over it can look like a mirror to an audience. Sometimes a bit of creative problem-solving can work stage miracles. In a scene that takes place by a roaring fire, a picture of a fire creates the illusion of one and the audience will easily go along with it.

READ PLAYS AND BOOKS ABOUT PLAY WRITING

Reading good plays is as interesting as watching them. By reading published plays you will learn a lot about the dramatic form (see appendix VIII). Children's plays generally deal with a single situation that relates to a child's experience.

Also, be sure to read books about play writing if you think plays are for you; this chapter is a mere introduction to the form to get you moving in the right direction (see appendix IV).

Go to theaters and see plays performed. Study the movements of the actors and how the dialogue is received by the audience. Note the details of the staging. If you can, join a local theater group and become involved in putting on a play. Even if you don't perform yourself, you can learn a lot as you help with sets, costumes, lighting, publicity, and so forth.

MARKETS

There are few markets existing solely for the publication of plays, but that means you can easily get to know the publishers and learn what each one requires.

Teenagers are quite capable of performing everything from Stephen Sondheim to Shakespeare, yet there is a demand for contemporary plays for junior and senior high school levels. Perhaps this is because costuming and staging for period pieces is more difficult to handle, or because royalties for performing Broadway hits are prohibitive for modest school budgets. But it may also be the strong need for young people to see themselves portrayed in contemporary situations, as Judy Blume's and Ann Martin's success in adolescent novels over the years has proved again and again. Most salable are light comedies, romances (no serious love scenes, however), and plays dealing with current family and school situations.

CHECKLIST—WRITING PLAYS

1. Choose a popular subject such as family, school, romance, or friendship.
2. Introduce the main character and hint at the plot right away.
3. Outline the bare bones of your play on paper to organize your thoughts and to balance the weight of each part.
4. Use the scenes of your play to structure your plot.
5. Assign visible characteristics to specific characters, but don't overdo it.
6. Use dialogue not only to keep the audience interested, but to give them information to advance your plot, or to tell what may be happening offstage or to other characters.
7. Keep things moving on stage. Have something going on that the audience can see.
8. Keep the production simple, using props, sets, and costumes that are easy to find or make.
9. Read and attend plays. Get involved in the production of a play if possible.
10. Get to know the markets for plays; there are few, so you can easily become an expert.

SUGGESTIONS—CHAPTER 14

1. Find a picture book story that you would like to turn into a play. What would you look for in judging whether it is a good candidate for this project?
2. Write a brief sketch, outlining your idea for a contemporary play for junior high or high school students based on some event in history. Figure out the cast of characters, the basic plot in one or two acts, the setting, and even some staging and props.

3. Write the opening scene of the play you sketched out in item 2, introducing the story line and the main character.

PLAY MENTIONED IN THIS CHAPTER

A Woman Called Truth, Sandra Fenichel Asher

PART FOUR

Selling Your Book

To sell stories, do three things:

1. Study your markets.
2. Get manuscripts in the mail.
3. Keep them there.

> —Dwight V. Swain, *Techniques of the Selling Writer*

15

Who Cares?

Queries and Proposals

Sending manuscripts to publishers is a time-consuming business. It is not unusual for an author to wait three or four months for a publisher to return a manuscript with a form letter saying "We regret that we cannot use your story at this time." No comment. No explanation.

At this rate, writers can grow old—and pretty cranky—before they have a thing in print. Is there a way to cut down this waiting time? Is there some way to find out if anyone is interested in your idea before you put in all the work and time? Yes, but it takes thought and planning.

SNIFF OUT THE COMPETITION

You may be so motivated to write your book that you won't stop to worry about whether someone else has done a book on the same topic, or with the same approach. That can lead to a lot of heartache later, when you learn that there are six other books similar to yours. Why would a publisher want to publish another one?

Stop a moment to look up your competition before you put in the serious work of writing or submitting a book to publishers. You can find other books on your topic by browsing online booksellers such as Book Sense, Amazon, or Barnes & Noble, or looking in the *Subject Guide to Children's Books in Print,* found in most libraries. Books are arranged under thousands of subject headings. With a little cross-checking, you can find other books in print on your subject.

WHO CARES?

It's tough to go it alone, without an agent, in these early days of your career especially with more and more publishers not accepting manuscripts directly from writers. However, your chances of finding an agent without having a finished book to show are almost nonexistent. Therefore, it makes sense to take action and learn how to get your work—particulary queries and proposals— to publishers on your own. Later, when you have a completed book to sell, you can look for an agent to help you place it and negotiate a contract.

Let's say that you are seriously interested in writing a nonfiction book about thunderstorms for readers eight to twelve years old. This will take a lot of research, so you need to know that a publisher will care about a book on this subject for this age group. In the *Subject Guide,* look up thunderstorms and all the cross-references you can think of: storms, lightning, meteorology, weather, and so on. Note whether the books listed are for the same general age range you're writing for. Track down those that you feel might be competitive to your book, at least in summaries or reviews, to see whether your book will be different enough for a publisher to be interested. Perhaps yours offers the most recent developments in technology, and the last book published on the topic does not include them. The date of publication is especially important in nonfiction, because new discoveries or methods can make your book valuable, even though there are other books on the subject. This could make a publisher take notice, because no other book for your target audience is as up to date as yours will be.

Subject matter isn't as crucial in a work of fiction, but it does matter. If there are already several picture books in print about a child losing a grandmother to Alzheimer's, for example, and yours is not significantly different in content or approach, it will have to stand out in some major way—exceptional writing, for example—for a publisher to want it.

Fiction or nonfiction, picture book or books for older readers, ask yourself how you can make your book unique so that an editor will want to buy it. If you can't come up with a terrific angle, or a narrower focus, or show that you have new information to offer, then you would be better off finding another topic.

A library with a small budget may not buy your book if it already has one on the subject, unless their current book is clearly out of date.

QUERY LETTER: STRAINING THE SYSTEM

Publishers receive large numbers of unsolicited manuscripts—those that come through the mails without an agent or a request from an editor—and it takes a lot of hours to log them in, read them, write up reports and recommendations, and possibly have a second reading. Some editors no longer accept unsolicited manuscripts because the numbers received have strained the system, outweighing the value of finding the occasional manuscript worth publishing.

Some editors will accept manuscripts from members of the Society of Children's Book Writers (see appendix VII) or from those who have heard them speak at various workshops and conferences because they feel these associations educate and inform writers in the proper presentation of material, which saves editorial staffs valuable time. Others ask that writers send in query letters instead of manuscripts, reducing the screening process to a manageable amount of time and effort. Thus, the query letter has become a standard part of the submission process.

The query letter was designed to eliminate wasted time for both you and the publisher. Everything about your query letter says something about you, so take it seriously. It is your introduction to the editor, so you want to present yourself as professionally as possible.

For picture books, you may not need a query letter at all. If the guidelines you find online at publishers' Web sites or in marketing guides (see chapter 18) tell you it's all right to do so, send the complete manuscript—up to about five or six pages—but if a query is requested, do your best to sum up the story or the concept in a paragraph. The process will weed out subjects in which the editor has no present interest. His declining your project does not mean your work is not good. Certain kinds of books, such as ABCs and nursery rhymes, dictionaries, and counting books, are already available in a variety of packaging, and many basic themes like wanting a best friend, or being afraid of the dark, may be turned down simply because there are too many like it already on the market.

For all other material, the query letter is a requirement of most publishers. From your study of publishers in chapter 3, you should be able to make up a list of those who might be interested in your idea. Write to them, simultaneously, asking if they would be interested in seeing your proposal or manuscript. At this point, you are just asking whether the subject matter would be of interest, so sending multiple inquiries is fine. Be sure to spell names correctly and get titles right.

SHOW YOU'RE ON THE BALL

Describe your book and explain why you find the subject fascinating, or why you feel qualified to write the book. Tell her why your book is needed in spite of the competition; perhaps it is more up to date technologically, or you will have personal experiences or interviews with experts in yours. Include any publishing credits you may have that seem appropriate—an article you wrote as a student for your school paper is not; an article for a magazine or newspaper to which the public subscribes is. Write an interesting, appealing opening relating to your topic to grab the editor's interest.

Note the other books in print on your subject for your age group and explain why your book could compete successfully with them. The point of finding other books is to show the editor to whom you are sending your work just what the competition is so she can evaluate your work in light of it. If she is interested, she will look it up herself, so show her you're on the ball.

SELL YOUR SUBJECT

Since you are unknown to the editor, you have to sell her on your subject rather than on yourself. Let's say you have written a novel that involves mental illness, and your experience of having a son with schizophrenia led you to write it. Include that because it gives you an advantage in having dealt personally with the subject of your book. Tell her anything that might be persuasive in stirring up interest, but avoid hard-sell tactics such as "This is the book you've been waiting for all your life!" which will probably be a turnoff.

Save It for Another Time

All of this should take no more than a one-page letter. The temptation will be to explain all about your project and yourself, but don't—save it for another time. Right now, you are simply trying to interest an editor in the subject matter, to show why you are the person for the job, and to weed out those publishers who have no interest in your book whatsoever, saving you (and them) a great deal of time and expense. Sending a query letter costs only the price of a first-class stamp, but mailing a manuscript costs far more.

When sending your query, enclose a stamped self-addressed envelope for the reply. Once you have responses to your letters (figure about four weeks for this, but it could take longer; all the more reason for sending several letters simultaneously), you will know which publishers want your manuscript or, for nonfiction, your detailed proposal.

As you study the guidelines offered by publishers, you will see that some just want query letters, others want a synopsis or sample chapters. Customize your query letter to accommodate each publisher.

Synopsis

If a synopsis is requested, as with fiction, this should include an overall summary of your book, no more than a page in length (unless specified otherwise), plus a chapter-by-chapter synopsis, with about two to three sentences per chapter, depending on the length of the book, showing your plan right up through the ending. This shows your ability to plot and to create good characters, and is the part of your submission that is of most interest to an editor.

Proposal

The proposal is a thoroughly prepared out presentation of the nonfiction book you have in mind. It should show the scope of the book you envision, and how it will be organized, including a

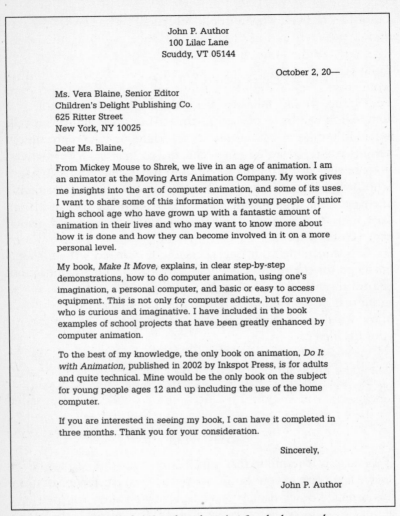

John P. Author
100 Lilac Lane
Scuddy, VT 05144

October 2, 20—

Ms. Vera Blaine, Senior Editor
Children's Delight Publishing Co.
625 Ritter Street
New York, NY 10025

Dear Ms. Blaine,

From Mickey Mouse to Shrek, we live in an age of animation. I am
an animator at the Moving Arts Animation Company. My work gives
me insights into the art of computer animation, and some of its uses.
I want to share some of this information with young people of junior
high school age who have grown up with a fantastic amount of
animation in their lives and who may want to know more about
how it is done and how they can become involved in it on a more
personal level.

My book, *Make It Move*, explains, in clear step-by-step
demonstrations, how to do computer animation, using one's
imagination, a personal computer, and basic or easy to access
equipment. This is not only for computer addicts, but for anyone
who is curious and imaginative. I have included in the book
examples of school projects that have been greatly enhanced by
computer animation.

To the best of my knowledge, the only book on animation, *Do It
with Animation*, published in 2002 by Inkspot Press, is for adults
and quite technical. Mine would be the only book on the subject
for young people ages 12 and up including the use of the home
computer.

If you are interested in seeing my book, I can have it completed in
three months. Thank you for your consideration.

Sincerely,

John P. Author

A query letter. Keep it brief and to the point for the best results.

detailed chapter breakdown, with a short paragraph for each
chapter. The proposal establishes your writing and research abilities. It can be sent out as soon as you receive a positive response
to your query letter. Sometimes several months will go by between query and proposal, in which case you might mention,
when you send the proposal, that you are following up on the
editor's response to a query made some time ago.

It is possible to sell a nonfiction book on the basis of a proposal. Your research need not be complete, but you must show the scope of the book, how you will approach your subject, and how you will organize your material. You will have to outline your material and complete a couple of sample chapters to show that you can write in depth about your subject.

For fiction, it is wise to finish your manuscript before submitting it unless you are working on a long and/or timely novel, or are a very slow writer, in which case you can put out some feelers while you are writing the second half of your book. Many publishers will accept a partial novel, but the success of fiction depends on plotting, pacing, suspense, characterization, and a satisfactory conclusion. A writer may have a good style and get off to a ripping start, but she can also lose her way halfway through a novel and never get back on track. For this reason, a partial novel is still only a sampling of your writing style; it will not lead to an offer of publication.

SAMPLE CHAPTERS

Sample chapters are not expected with a query letter, unless the publisher's guidelines tell you otherwise. Sample chapters are generally sent when a publisher has responded positively to your query, and you are following up with either a detailed proposal or the whole book.

Which part of the manuscript should you send, or how many chapters? It depends on whether it is fiction or nonfiction. Always send the beginning chapters of a novel. Pay special attention to your opening page or pages, which is the first opportunity for the editor to become interested and be drawn into the drama that is to unfold. If you've hooked the editor at the beginning, that's a good sign.

Nonfiction is usually outlined carefully and sent with a couple of sample chapters. You will probably want to send the first chapter, which introduces the subject and shows how you will deal with the subject in the rest of your book, and another chapter that shows off some really interesting aspect of your book that you have researched and also displays your best writing. An active chapter, with good tension, where something exciting is happening in the development of your topic, is a good choice.

ABRACADABRA!

Creating Your Own Magic Show from Beginning to End

by Barbara Seuling

CHAPTER I—YOU THE MAGNIFICENT

This chapter deals with creating the image of someone with
special, magical, powers. Adopting some sort of name, such
as "Alan the Amazing" or "The Mystifying Markwell." Creating
a costume to go with the image: clown, formal, swami, wizard.
Directions for making simple costumes without sewing. What
it takes to convince an audience of your magical abilities.
Concentration. Self-confidence. The need for good props.
Developing good practice habits. Having a goal, like putting
on a magic show.

CHAPTER II—A MAGICIAN'S SECRETS

In addition to regular, easy-to-come-by props such as glasses,
a plate, string, and a deck of cards, and even some larger
items such as two chairs and a curtain, there are props
very special to a magician. These look ordinary—envelopes,
newspapers, cereal boxes—but the magician has "treated"
them so that he may perform "magic" when using them.
This chapter goes into the careful preparation of certain props
which are needed for the tricks in Chapter III. They can be
made with everyday objects found around the house. Perhaps
also a paragraph on why magic "works."

CHAPTER III—YOUR BAG OF TRICKS

The most fascinating types of magic tricks described in detail.
Step-by-step instructions and illustrations. These ten tricks
will form the basis for the reader's magic show. Another
chapter deals with making the props for some of these tricks.

*A sample proposal. This was for a book on magic that had to compete
with lots of others still in print. I had to come up with something unusual.
I added a section on putting on a magic show. Mixing magic tricks and
showmanship seemed to work. The editor bought the project. As the book
got under way, it became clear that there was too much material in
chapter III, "Your Bag of Tricks," so it was subsequently divided into
two parts: "Warm-ups and Relaxers," and "Razzlers and Dazzlers."*

Each trick will have a snappy title. Further reading suggestions will be made, as there are a number of good books on magic tricks and how to do them. Tricks include: making something disappear; sawing someone in half; changing one thing into another; pulling something out of the air; guessing something using ESP; having something put itself back together after breaking or ripping it apart; an escape trick; a card trick; pushing one solid object through another solid object.

CHAPTER IV—PRESENTING . . . YOUR MAGIC SHOW!

Once tricks are practiced and mastered, props are in good working order, costume and image have been worked out, and the reader is ready to perform in front of an audience, he or she will need some pointers. First, there is publicity. Sample tickets are shown, which the reader can make himself. A word about advertising, including posters. How to attract an audience. Starting with a few people and building up to larger groups. Sample routines and programs for all occasions. Suggestions for accompanying music. Having an assistant. Staging and sets. A monogram, or signature, of the "star." A grand finale.

Magic Dealers

Magic Publications

Books about Stage Magic

Index

It is sometimes feasible to send only one sample chapter with your outline, depending on the publisher's requirements, the length of your book, and the subject matter. However, a single chapter is not enough for most editors to judge the worth of the entire manuscript, especially if it is the first chapter, which is usually an introduction to your subject. So if you write only one sample chapter, get into the heart of your subject; choose a part of the book that is especially interesting for you. Your enthusiasm will be more constant and your writing will be at its best if you truly enjoy the material. If you send two chapters, one of them can be the first chapter, but the second can be from the meatier middle.

OVERALL VIEW

In a cover letter give an overall view of the book and your credentials. You do not have to be an expert on the topic, but if there is any special connection between you and your subject, let the editor know about your position of insight and experience. When presenting a book of mathematical puzzles and pastimes, for example, it can help to indicate that you are a high school math teacher. Similarly, making the editor aware that a book on the natural history of the raccoon is by someone who has spent the last four years as a country veterinarian can be important.

If you have special resources at your disposal to research your subject from a closer or more unusual angle than other books on the subject, submit that in your proposal.

BE PASSIONATE

Tell the editor the age group for which you intend the book and why your particular approach is going to make a difference. If you have chosen your subject well, then you are enthusiastic about it; let that enthusiasm come through. The editor will feel it, and that can work in your favor. There is nothing as appealing as an author who is excited about her work.

Avoid writing about subjects simply because they are "in" or there is a "need" for books about them; you will only add to the dross in publishers' offices, the hundreds of unpublishable manuscripts, pedantic and dull, that come in from people who believe that wanting to write for children or liking a subject is enough. You must be passionate about your subject.

I remember, as an editor, what fun it was when an author came to see me, spilling over with the joy of his discoveries as he researched and wrote his latest book. Even if the subject would otherwise have left me cold, this enthusiasm would be contagious, and I would be swept along. I was so ignorant of sports when I started out, it was pathetic. Yet I inherited a popular sports writer who was in the middle of a book on football when his editor left the company. I didn't know what the term *conversion* meant; I hardly knew the rules of the game. But I quickly became engrossed in the subject while I was working with him, because he made it alive and interesting with his own enthusiasm.

SELECT FEW

Proposals may be sent out to more than one publisher at a time, but you must make it clear you are doing that. The guidelines will tell you whether or not a publisher accepts multiple submissions. If he doesn't, put him on a separate list. You will have to wait to hear from him before you send your proposal out again. This could take a lot of time, but may be well worth it to work with your desired publisher or editor.

To gain an editor's interest and appreciation, you may find it useful to allow for an exclusive period of time—two or three weeks—with a particular publisher, before making your proposal available to others. Make it clear in your cover letter that you are doing this and say why. It is not a bad idea to let an editor know that you have singled her out because you admire another book that she edited, or that you like the quality of the publisher's books. That shows that you have done some research and are not choosing her at random.

The closest thing to a proposal for a picture book is when an illustrator with a picture book idea presents a dummy book and a color reproduction of one finished illustration. This procedure is covered in detail in chapter 17, "For the Writer Who Is Also an Illustrator." If you are not an illustrator, the dummy is not necessary for submitting work. Your manuscript must speak for you in terms of your ability as a writer of picture books. Do not add notations to your manuscript about how you think the illustrations should look unless absolutely necessary.

For example, if there is an element in your story that is essential visually but not written into the text, as in Ellen Raskin's *Nothing Ever Happens on My Block*, where a boy laments that nothing ever happens on his block, yet behind his back some very dramatic events are taking place, you would have to note it.

In all your mailings, remember the SASE (self-addressed stamped envelope). It should become second nature to enclose one whenever you send anything to a publisher: request for guidelines, query letter, proposal, or manuscript. As a writer, you will need plenty of these, so you may want to prepare a good supply of them in advance, and hope that one day one of them comes back to you with an offer of a contract inside.

SUGGESTIONS—CHAPTER 15

1. Write a query letter. Choose one of the hypothetical subjects below as though it were your own idea. Don't forget to check the competition.
    a. Searching for dinosaurs; nonfiction, ages 8 to 12
    b. Looking for signs of life on Mars; nonfiction, age 12 and up
    c. The adventure of a cabin boy who joins the crew of a whaling ship; fiction, ages 8 to 12
    d. Teenage fiction about a girl who has an eating disorder, age 12 and up
    e. A story about a lost duckling; fiction picture book, ages 4 to 7
2. List six publishers to whom you would send your query. Why do you feel these houses are the ones most likely to respond positively to your hypothetical book?
3. Research agents and list three whom you feel you might want to represent you. What is your reason for each of your choices?

BOOKS MENTIONED IN THIS CHAPTER
(IN ORDER OF APPEARANCE)

Subject Guide to Children's Books in Print, R. R. Bowker
Nothing Ever Happens on My Block, Ellen Raskin

16

Submitting Your Manuscript
Presenting Yourself to a Publisher

It is at this point that those ads in the writers' magazines stating "We are looking for writers like you" and "Let us publish your manuscript" begin to look appealing. Why go through all this bother and hard work? If you want your book in print so badly, why not go to one of these companies?

Simply stated, this is not traditional publishing. The publishers who run these ads may be subsidy or vanity publishers. There is more about this in chapter 19, explaining the differences. For now, let's concentrate on the path more commonly taken to get a book published—where you get paid for your manuscript and the publisher pays all the expenses.

AGENTS

You have a manuscript completed. It has been read at your critique group, revised, sent to a freelance editor, revised again, and it is ready to submit. Do you go directly to your market guide and find the publishers to send it to, or do you get an agent?

All writers come to this question at one point or another. Before you decide, consider what agents can do for you. You know, of course, that agents send your manuscript to publishers, hoping for a sale. And naturally, they try to match you to the right one. Agents are more in tune with the publishing industry than most writers and in a good position to find the right editor at the right publishing house. You know, too, that agents have access to publishers that you may not.

They negotiate, using their vast knowledge of the publishing industry and their personal experience with various houses, to not just take what is offered but to get you the best deal possible. They see that their clients receive competitive advances, whereas beginners might accept less because they are so eager to be published and don't know how to value their own work.

Agents protect your rights, seeing to it that you get a good contract and a fair share of income from your book. Agents keep your career moving forward, managing your schedule and repositioning you with different houses as you advance and need them. They are your advocate when issues arise with the editor or publisher, and support you emotionally when you're going through tough times.

Agents do much more, or less, depending on their style. Some will act as editors and work with you on your book until they feel it is ready to submit to a publisher; others will never get involved in the editorial process. Some will become friends and be involved in your life, while others will keep a professional distance. There are agents who are content to handle everything for you and leave you to your writing, and others who prefer that you work with them in active ways to promote your career. Some agents don't mind if you have contact with editors and come back to them when it's time to negotiate a contract; others want to drive the deal from the beginning and only want you to get involved after contract talks have begun.

While writers may sometimes have gripes about agents who did or did not do what they thought the agents should do, for the most part, writers have a trusting, close relationship with their agents. Some have even become like family.

When agent Marilyn Marlow died in 2003, scores of clients mourned her, along with just about everyone in the children's book business. Marlow had been the agent to many well-known stars of the children's book world, some of them from their first book. She had nurtured and scolded them, protected them from bad contracts and impossible schedules, pushed them forward to shine brighter, fought for their rights and better terms. But the stories told about her at her memorial service in New York were about Marlow on a shopping trip when someone on her staff had a baby, or a memorable visit she made to a client's home in the country, or the time she baby-sat their children. Most could not figure out how to move on without Marilyn guiding their lives.

Finding an agent is not that easy. It's pretty much the same routine as finding a publisher. Do your research and find out what you can about different agents. Query to see if the ones you think you'd like to work with are available and willing to consider representing you. If they are open to new clients, send your manuscript and wait for a response. If you get a positive response and it is the right agent for you, then move ahead with a contract. If not, try the next agent.

Newer agents who are still building a client list might be more willing to take on an unknown, unproved writer. Check the agent's credentials and ask to see his client list of published authors. Find out if he charges a reading fee; those who are members of the Association of Author Representatives do not, as part of their canon of ethics.

You may have to go it alone for a while, until you have sold a book on your own. It is even conceivable that you could phone an agent the minute an editor nibbles at your manuscript, and have the agent step in at that point to negotiate. Agent Scott Treimel strongly recommends that if you do this, do not commit to anything before the agent comes in. Tell the publisher you have to think it over and will get back to him. The agent with a free hand can work a far better deal than if he's taking on a situation in which you have already conceded certain points.

Agents will charge you the standard 15 percent commission, tax deductible, to represent you. For all that they do, this is not only fair but is probably more than made up for in the deals they can get for you.

You will find agents listed in various marketing directories (see appendix V) and books. Only patience and research will help you find the one that's right for you (appendix IV).

On Your Own

Being on your own, whether by choice or necessity, is difficult but certainly doable. You have to work hard and be smart. You must be willing to learn about markets and submitting procedures, keep excellent records about the status of every manuscript you have circulating, and track comments received. You must familiarize yourself with publishers' lists and the people who run them so you can remain personally involved in contacting editors and evaluating their responses.

You must be knowledgeable about contract terms and money. You can hire a lawyer to read your contract and explain it to you, but the lawyer should have book contract experience. A lawyer can protect your rights, but he has to know what they are and what's negotiable and the percentage of income you might expect with the sale of various rights.

While many of the major publishers are no longer accepting unsolicited manuscripts, some houses still do. You have to seek them out and familiarize yourself with them. You also have to find any legal and ethical method to reach those who have, essentially, closed their doors. No editor will turn away someone who has been referred to him by one of his published authors, so if you are lucky enough to have that connection, use it.

Editors who speak at writers' conferences and workshops you attend will usually look at work you send to them following that event.

Several major publishers sponsor contests with publication as a prize. Having your manuscript read for a contest gets you in the door of a publisher who may not accept your manuscript otherwise.

Write query letters if they are required; and when you receive positive responses, follow up by sending your manuscript in a reasonable amount of time.

Send your work to small houses. Their advances are not as large as those offered by the bigger houses, but your main goal at the beginning of your career is to get published and establish yourself as a writer. You probably will also receive more attention at a smaller house, where there are fewer books and authors.

Knowing your way around publishers and editors, and keeping current on the latest news in the publishing industry will give you important working tools to sell your own work and, if you decide at some later point to work with an agent, you will be a more valuable client, who can be actively involved in your own career.

FORMATTING YOUR MANUSCRIPT

In the near future it may be totally acceptable to transmit work without ever having to print it on paper or use a stamp, but for now it is only after a manuscript is accepted that the editor will ask for work to be submitted via e-mail. Other editors may ask for both an electronic copy and a manuscript; it varies from publisher to publisher.

Use twenty-pound white bond paper (not the erasable kind if you're still using a typewriter), 8½ by 11 inches. Identify the work with a cover page that includes your book title and your name, address, telephone number, and e-mail address or that of your agent, if you have one. This page identifies your work and also serves as protection; if it gets soiled and has to be replaced, it's not a big deal, and you only have to reprint or type just that page, not the manuscript. Use one side of the paper only. Double-space your text and indent five or six spaces for paragraphs. Leave about 1½ inches at the bottom, and at least an inch for the left and right margins.

Picture book manuscripts should be printed on full pages (not as you visualize the final book, with only three or four lines to a page). Do not indicate illustration breaks; this is the editor's job.

In the upper left corner on page one, identify your work with your name and address, and in the upper right corner, show the approximate total number of words (to the nearest fifty). Your title, centered and in upper case, goes halfway down the page. Four lines below the title, type the first line of the text.

Your last name and an identifying word or two from your title should appear in the upper left corner of each remaining manuscript page. Number the pages of the manuscript consecutively throughout, not chapter by chapter.

MAKING CORRECTIONS

Check your manuscript carefully for errors. Use a spell checker and a grammar checker, if you can. Two or three inked changes in a 120-page manuscript are all right, but more will make your manuscript look sloppy.

John P. Author
100 Lilac Lane
Scuddy, VT 05144

[approximate number of words]

TITLE OF STORY

This is how your manuscript should look when it is presented to an editor. Your paper should be 8-1/2 x 11-inch white bond, preferably with some rag content, for durability, and no lighter than 20-pound weight. Be sure to set your printer to "normal" quality, rather than draft for a dark, clean copy.

Type your complete name and address in the upper-left corner and an approximate word count in the upper right. (There are about 250 words per double-spaced typed or printed page, using standard twelve-point type.)

Your title should be typed one-third to halfway down the first page, centered, all in upper case. Under the title, type your name in upper and lower case. (This is optional if it is at the top left of the page.) The first page is not numbered, but subsequent pages are. Identify each page with your last name and a key word from the title, in the upper-left corner. Text from page two on (except for chapter beginnings) begins about 1 1/2 inches from the top. Each new chapter begins on a new page, halfway down the page.

This is standard manuscript format. After a while, you will know how to do it without looking at the sample, but until you do, use it whenever you prepare a manuscript for submission to an agent or an editor.

Author/STORY

Type on one side of the paper only, double-spaced. Indent five or six spaces for paragraphs. Do not staple or bind pages together. A paper clip is okay, as long as the pages are easy to separate during a reading.

You can fold a short manuscript (one to four pages) in thirds and mail it in a no. 10 letter-size envelope. Longer manuscripts should be mailed, unfolded, in 9 by 11-inch envelopes. Use your judgment on whether or not it needs a stiff cardboard backing for stability.

Always include a self-addressed stamped envelope with sufficient postage for the return of your manuscript.

Address your manuscript, with a brief cover letter, to a person, not just a department. You can find the names of editors in various publishing directions, such as the annual *Children's Writer's and Illustrator's Market* (see appendix V).

COVER LETTER

A cover letter is not necessary, but it's courteous, like a hand-shake. Address a person, not a department, and get the titles right. Spell names correctly. A phone call or an online check only takes a minute and can make the difference between being read or tossed. If you do send a letter, keep it brief. Never give a synopsis of your story or explain your work in a letter accompanying a manuscript; the work should explain itself. If it needs help, it isn't ready to be sent out. Include the title of your work, any publishing credits, and reference to any previous query.

Listings of agents, publishing houses, and individual editors appear in various marketing guides and newslettters (see appendix V).

EXTRA MATTER

When you submit a book with sidebars or extra matter that is not in the actual text, add it by way of additional pages at the end of your manuscript; don't try to incorporate it into the main body of the manuscript. The editor, in consultation with the illustrator and book designer, will decide how and where to include it.

WHEN IT'S READY TO GO

If your manuscript is one to four pages long, you can fold it in thirds and put it in a regular business-size (no. 10) envelope, or a 5 by 7-inch manila envelope, for a picture book manuscript. A no. 10 envelope may go astray, into the regular mail, instead of with the manuscripts, adding unnecessarily to your waiting time. If you use the manila envelope, fold the manuscript in half. Up to ten pages can fit neatly into this package. Anything longer should not be folded. Use a larger manila envelope and a piece of cardboard to keep the pages from being bent or folded in transit. Do not use report covers or any binding; editors prefer loose, separate pages. A simple paper clip holding the pages together is acceptable.

For manuscripts more than one hundred pages long, it is advisable to use a cardboard mailing box. These can be found in most stationery stores. The box protects the corners of your manuscript from becoming dog-eared in everyday handling and from rattling around in post offices and mail rooms. A trick to keeping your manuscript looking fresh is to print new copies of worn-looking pages before sending it out again.

Include a self-addressed envelope with sufficient return postage for everything you send out, from query letter to final manuscript. Manuscripts without appropriate postage will not be returned.

No doubt, with so many writers using word processors that can spit out copies cheaply and easily, it would probably be more economical to ask the agent or publisher not to return your manuscript, but to dispose of it instead. That would save you return postage, too, except for the price of a letter telling you the editor's decision. There are ecological considerations, too; think of all that wasted paper! Publishers and writers may one day adopt a system whereby manuscripts can be disposed of responsibly, by sending them to a paper recycling plant. Some houses already do this with in-house paper. Meanwhile, the traditional method of sending return postage for manuscripts still applies.

If your manuscript is peculiar in shape, size, or bulk, have it sent to the publisher by special mail service, packaged with care, and with complete instructions and postage for its return. If you live near a publisher, you can arrange by phone to deliver and retrieve the manuscript yourself.

Don't Send Illustrations

It is not a good idea to send artwork with your manuscript. The text alone is what the editor wants to judge. Never have an outside artist do illustrations for your book. I emphasize this because I want to be sure you understand it. I can't tell you how many beginning writers are under the impression that they must provide illustrations for their picture book texts. An editor will provide for illustrations if he buys your text. If you are an illustrator or work closely with a collaborator, you may send along a couple of sketches and a copy of finished art; the editor will look at these. It is still your text that is under consideration, however, and illustrations will not make up for what is lacking there. Many writers send out material before it is ready, yet include artwork for it; perhaps they feel more comfortable hiding behind pictures. The sad thing is that, if anything, it tends to put the text under closer scrutiny in the editor's effort to overcome any influence that the art may impose. The more appropriate method for showing illustrations, yours or someone else's, is to show samples of your work to an art director, independently of text. See chapter 17 for details of this procedure.

POSTAGE

Postage requirements change from time to time; you should consult the domestic mail manual, available at all post offices, or online at www.usps.com for current rates and rules. Mail clerks are not always knowledgeable about such things as manuscripts, so do the looking yourself. The current manuscript rate may change but, hopefully, there will always be some inexpensive way of sending original manuscripts through the mail.

Once writers are sending disks rather than manuscripts to publishers as a matter of course, postage costs will be much more affordable. First-class mail is fast, but it can be expensive after a few mailings, especially if your manuscript is a 200-page novel. Media mail is cheaper, but it takes longer. Disks are as light as a letter.

ROUTING THE MANUSCRIPT

Keeping up with those trade publications and publishers' catalogs now begins to pay off. You should have a good sense of where you are going to send your manuscript. It should not take much brushing up to prepare a list of the agents or publishers most likely to respond favorably to it. If you are following up a query, the publishers who said they would look at your manuscript are already set out for you.

Make up a routing slip showing the title of your work, the publisher to whom you sent it, the date on which you mailed it and, if you receive an acknowledgment, the date it was received at the publishing house.

Leave space for the date that you receive the manuscript back and any remarks or comments. Once a contract is offered, you may keep other records; this is just to show where your manuscript is at any time, and to keep track of who has seen it.

Some people enclose a preprinted self-addressed, and stamped postcard along with the manuscript. This does not guarantee a response, but makes it a little easier for the publisher to acknowledge receipt of your manuscript.

WAITING FOR A DECISION

You will probably wait a long time for the publisher's decision. The time varies from house to house, and can be up to several months per publisher. Small houses with small staffs generally take a lot longer to make decisions than large houses with lots of readers. After three months, follow up your submission with a query about whether your manuscript is still under consideration.

MULTIPLE SUBMISSIONS

Is it okay to send the same manuscipt to several publishers at the same time? Yes, but be aware that some editors cling to tradition like a life preserver, and the tradition some years ago was that manuscripts were submitted to one publisher at a time. As waiting time for decisions increased dramatically, it became a hardship for anyone trying to earn a living by writing, and the custom gave way to submitting to several houses at a time. As Judith Mathews pointed out in her letter in the *Society of Children's Book Writers & Illustrators Bulletin*, there is no other industry that requires a person to sell his product to only one potential customer at a time, while also forcing that seller to wait months for a decision. Marketing directories indicate whether a house embraces the practice of multiple submissions or not. With these as your guide, you will be able to submit your work to as many

Date _____

Dear Mr. Author,

This acknowledges receipt by this department of your manuscript, *Great Day in the Morning*.

Sincerely,

_____

Children's Delight Publishing Co.

Although there is no guarantee, it may hurry things along for you and the publisher if you enclose a stamped self-addressed acknowledgment postcard with your manuscript.

publishers as you like. If you want to give a publisher exclusivity for a set time, because you have a special feeling for that house, say so in your cover letter and follow up when you say you will.

BOOK PACKAGERS

Packagers or book producers may act as your agent and take a commission out of your fee, should they hire you for a writing assignment.

Book producers or packagers are companies that pitch ideas for projects—single title or series—to publishers as a total package. They can provide everything from the series' identity, the authors and illustrators, all the work of the production process, to finished books, if that's what the publisher wants. If you submit work to a packager, you automatically agree to having the packager represent you, as an agent, along with your work. Contracts are often negotiated in groups of three or four books at a time; if the first titles sell well, more books will be added to the series. Single books can be considered, but it's the multibook package that is most economical for the packager. Sometimes a packager comes up with the idea and several writers are hired to write under a single pen name for that series, because books are produced at a rapid rate—once a month is not uncommon—too fast for most writers to create single-handedly.

Be sure to read your contract and understand the terms before you sign anything.

INTEREST IN FURTHER WORK

It sometimes happens that an editor will ask to see further work, even if the present submission cannot be used. Be sure to follow up on this; if you are fortunate enough to receive comments of any sort about your writing, even an indication of interest in your style, you would be wasting a real opportunity to let it pass you by. If you should receive suggestions on how to revise your work, be sure to send the revised manuscript back to the editor who made the suggestions unless it is made clear you should not. Use every opportunity that comes your way.

COPYRIGHT

I have never personally known of a case of anyone's idea being stolen in the process of submitting work to a publisher. Beginning writers seem to have a preoccupation with this notion and go to great lengths to protect their manuscripts. The fact is, you cannot copyright an idea—and for good reason. Ideas are duplicated all the time. It is the execution of those ideas that makes a work unique. Think of all those Renaissance Madonnas, for example, and how many artists worked on the same theme, relentlessly, and yet no two are alike. Writers often come up with exciting and wonderful ideas only to find that someone else has already thought of them, or to learn that three publishers are coming out with books on the same subject in the next publishing season. There is nothing to be done; duplication of ideas is bound to occur.

The copyright law protects your work from the moment it is in "fixed form." This means once you have your story in manuscript form, or even a good outline, you are protected automatically. Your records, such as your routing record, should be sufficient evidence of the date of ownership. Forms for official copyright registration may be obtained from the Copyright Office of the Library of Congress in Washington, D.C., but when a manuscript is purchased, it is not necessary to apply for copyright yourself. Your publisher will do that for you, in your name, on publication of your book.

Two exceptions to that rule come to mind. First, for an existing series developed by the publisher, copyright is generally taken in the name of the publisher or creator of the series. Also, when a writer does work for hire the work may be part of a larger project which is copyrighted by the owner of it.

If you give up your rights to a work for any reason, you may request the reversion of rights once that work has been out of print for a period of time.

You are now taking a very important step in your journey into children's book publishing, and the hard part, the waiting, has yet to begin. There is only one way I know to make this time pass more easily, and that is to get going on your next project. Start a new book or story or article. Get completely involved with a whole new set of problems, characters, and situations. The time will pass a lot more quickly, and you will be less anxious about the work that is out. More important, you will prove that you are a writer by getting on with your work.

SUGGESTIONS—CHAPTER 16

1. Look up the latest information on copyright with the Copyright Office and send for the literature available.
2. Make up a file for your routing records. Design a routing sheet or page to be filled out each time you send out a manuscript or receive it back, showing the date, the publisher, the title of the manuscript, and anything else that will be helpful to you at a glance, like age of reader or type of manuscript.

ORGANIZATIONS MENTIONED IN THIS CHAPTER

Association of Author Representatives (AAR)
    http://www.aar-online.org
Society of Children's Book Writers and Illustrators (SCBWI)
    http://www.scbwi.org

17

For the Writer Who Is Also an Illustrator

What the Illustrator Needs to Know

Although this is a book for the writer, this chapter is included for those who draw or paint as well as write, and whose artwork is inseparable from their writing.

To illustrate books your work must be of professional quality. It isn't enough just to "draw a little." If your writing is polished and ready to submit but your artwork is not, it is better to show yourself as a writer first, and wait until you are ready to show your art.

As an illustrator, you must have the ability to handle the technical skills required, such as drawing, handling various media, preparing a storyboard, making a dummy book, preparing camera-ready art, and being able to tell a story visually. As an illustrator you should have at least a familiarity with production techniques and have the ability to lay out a picture book in a balanced way, relating pictures to text in a smooth, interesting, and attractive fashion.

When you are the creator of both text and pictures for a proposed picture book, send the following to the children's book editor at the publishing house of your choice:

1. *A typed or printed manuscript.* The manuscript should be presented separately from the one you cut up to paste in your dummy. Do not use fancy fonts, varying sizes, or bold type. Don't break up the manuscript as you would in a book; it should be one continuous text.

2. *A copy of one piece of finished art.* Do not send the original. A good color reproduction is fine for this purpose. The illustration should be representative of your style and ability. If there are children or animals in your book, have them in your sample in an active, rather than passive, scene.

3. *A dummy book.* Make up a dummy in the size you feel is right for your book. Use drawing or visualizing paper for this, and attach a cover made of heavier paper or cardboard. Sketch in the illustrations in black and white where you feel they should go. Indicate with ruled lines or printed copy where the text will fit on the page. Leave plenty of white or light background space for the text. Work up a cover design for the book, in color. Although it does not have to be finished art, it should represent the book and show you at your best. The dummy shows your ability to design a picture book to flow from spread to spread. Remember to use the appropriate number of pages—thirty-two is the usual number for a picture book, although some are produced with forty-eight. It's a matter of economics. Picture books are printed on both sides of a single press sheet. With careful placement of art, plus cutting and folding, the sheet is turned into groups of folded printed pages, called signatures, which are later sewn together and bound. Keeping the printing to a single press sheet keeps the price of the finished book within bounds for the average book buyer.

End papers, the decorative pages at either end of the book that are pasted down to the book's cover, can be part of the book pages, and therefore printed with art, or paper—white or colored—can be added separately at the time of binding. In the latter case, all thirty-two pages can then be used for text and art. Remember to allow for the front matter (dedication, title page, copyright notice, and so forth) and back matter (author biography, notes on the production—whatever the publisher wants to include). (See the example of a dummy book in chapter 8.)

Any medium or reproducible technique that suits the type of book you are doing is acceptable. Experiment. Mary Azarian won the coveted Caldecott Medal in 1999 for her woodcuts in *Snowflake Bentley,* written by Jacqueline Briggs Martin, a picture book portraying strong Vermont characters. Chris Van Allsburg illustrated the 1982 Caldecott winner, *Jumanji,* entirely in pencil.

Simms Taback used gouache, watercolor, pencil, ink, clippings from magazines and photographs, and die-cut holes to illustrate his Caldecott award-winning children's book, *Joseph Had a Little Overcoat* in 2000. And in 2003, *Kogi's Mysterious Journey,* a picture book by Elizabeth Partridge, was illustrated by Aki Sogabe using all cut-paper illustrations.

A cautionary note: paints do not reproduce as accurately as inks. Inks are absorbed into the paper but paints lay on the surface, which means they reflect light differently. A reproduction from inks is always more accurate to the eye. Printers can match inks to inks better than to paints for this reason. Permanent markers are like ink when fresh, but the colors tend to fade rather quickly; keep work done in markers out of strong light.

In the last decade, more and more picture book illustrators have utilized the computer to create or enhance their illustrations. Revolutionary software for Mac computers can produce work that looks amazingly like traditionally rendered art, using sophisticated programs like Adobe Photoshop or Fractal Design Painter and a digital drawing pad with a stylus. The results can be spectacular, as evidenced in books like *Red Racer* by Audrey Wood and *Cock-a-Doodle-Do* by Janet Stevens. While it's not a medium for everyone, the computer has become another tool of the artist for creating picture books.

When you are hired to illustrate a book, your own or someone else's, you will discuss it with the editor or art director. First, you will create sketches that show your style and plan for the layout of the book. You will make a storyboard or dummy book or maybe both. You will talk about your technique, the book's jacket, size, and shape, color, and anything else that affects the look of the book. You will also have a deadline, or delivery date for the finished art. The art director, rather than the editor, will be your best pal during this time, should any problems or questions arise, although most editors keep a close watch on all stages of the book.

STORYBOARD

The storyboard is the rough plan of how you will lay out the book and distribute the illustrations. You make a storyboard by ruling the outlines of your pages, smaller than but in proportion

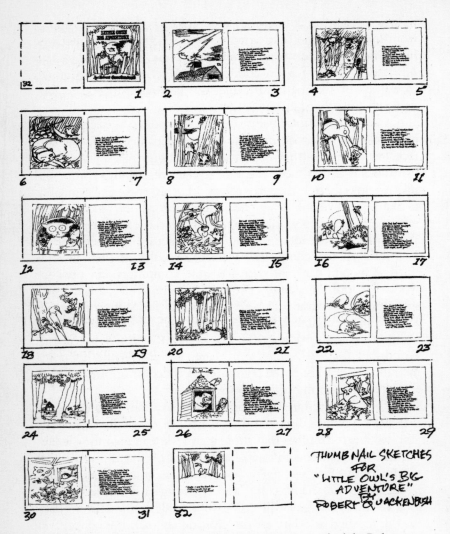

First stage thumbnail sketches for a thirty-two-page picture book by Robert Quackenbush, originally titled Little Owl's Big Adventure. From these sketches a book evolved titled Batbaby (Random House 1997), winner of a Gradiva Award for the best juvenile book of 1998, and its sequel Batbaby Finds a Home (Random House 2001). Used by permission of the author. All rights reserved.

to your proposed page size, on a large sheet of paper or illustration board. Keep in mind that traditional sizes, such as an upright 8 by 10-inch book, or an oblong 7 by 10-inch book, are more economical for the publisher than an odd size. Roughly sketch in each picture and where the text will fit on the pages. Color is not necessary, but it may be helpful in seeing how your color moves throughout the book. The storyboard is discussed with the editor and art director before proceeding with full-size sketches.

DUMMY BOOK

Sketches are worked out to show more detail, but they are rough, not finished illustrations. Placement of elements and characterization are important at this stage. A dummy book is sometimes made up with the sketches in place. Decide on the size of your book. Using visualizing paper—it comes in pads—make two signatures, of eight pages each, folded in half. Trim these to the size you want. Stitch each signature along the crease, then tie or stitch them to each other. Make a cover for this out of heavier paper, which can be pasted to thin cardboard for a sturdier construction. Allow room in your thirty-two-page design for the title page, copyright notice, and dedication.

Color is indicated in at least some of the illustrations at this time and hand-lettered or printed copy is pasted in place. The editor and art director go over the dummy for content, continuity, color, and logic. When the work gets final approval, you proceed with finished art.

MASTER YOUR SKILLS

It is necessary to state once again that unless your artwork is of professional quality, you should send your manuscript without pictures. The demands on even the most talented illustrator are great. If you have mastered certain skills, you will be able to meet the challenges. If you feel any doubts about your abilities, yet know you have the talent, brush up on your skills. Courses are offered in extension systems, colleges, and art schools everywhere.

Today I am a dragon.
My face is scary.
My claws are very sharp.

These are pages from a dummy book. You don't have to be an artist to need a dummy as a working tool when writing a picture book, but it will help you balance the text. Remember to include a variety of illustration possibilities, and keep the action moving forward.

I can make fire come out
of my nose.

Even an assistant's job in the graphics department of a large company or a design studio will put you in touch with state-of-the-art equipment and techniques. A professional illustrator who lives in your area might be willing to tutor you in basic illustration techniques, picture book layout, or whatever specifics you need to know. There are also a number of good books available by illustrators who share their experiences with you (see appendix VI). Once you have mastered the essentials, you will learn by experience. Take smaller jobs until you get your feet wet. Learn the procedures of working with a publisher. The more you understand about the process of picture book making the better you will be to meet the challenges you face.

STUDY OTHER ILLUSTRATORS

In addition to availing yourself of the traditional methods of training, study the works of other illustrators, past and present, not to copy them but to learn from them. By all means, study the latest picture books by Vera Williams, Peter Sis, Jan Brett, Chris Van Allsburg, Brian Pinkney, and Christopher Myers. But go back a step, too, to the work of illustrators who only a few years ago set standards for today's illustrators: Maurice Sendak, Eric Carle, Uri Shulevitz, Leo and Diane Dillon, Barbara Cooney, Arnold Lobel, and Ezra Jack Keats. Don't limit yourself to only the most recent books if you want to do a major study in craftsmanship. Keep your mind and eyes open to a wide range of illustration styles. A well-stocked children's bookstore is a good place to see the latest books, but libraries will undoubtedly have some of the longlasting old favorites.

It is realistic to say that, as a beginner, you will find it difficult to get a job illustrating a picture book. As an unknown, you are competing with professionals who are sure to sell more books for the publisher on the recognition of their names alone. Jacket illustration, spot drawings, and black-and-white illustrations for early chapter books are places where you can best find your first professional work. These jobs, in turn, can help you land meatier illustration assignments and, hopefully, your first picture book contract.

SHOW YOUR WORK

If you have a portfolio of illustrations to show (and you should, if you want a career as an illustrator), you can benefit from a publication offered by the Children's Book Council—free for a self-addressed stamped (postage for 3 ounces) envelope—called "An Illustrator's Guide to Members of the Children's Book Council." It tells you, in addition to the name, address, telephone number, and contact person at each publishing house, how to arrange an appointment to have your work seen. It also tells you what to do if you cannot come in in person, and what a publisher wants to see. (See the appendixes for references to books, organizations, and conferences where you can have your work seen by professionals.)

The illustrator of a picture book receives a share of the royalties depending on her contribution to the whole book. These rates vary, but on picture books the illustrator generally shares fifty-fifty with the author. If you do both text and illustrations you will get to keep the entire royalty.

SUGGESTIONS—CHAPTER 17

1. Prepare a storyboard for a familiar folk tale, such as *Jack and the Beanstalk*. Are the end papers included in your layout or will they be added separately?
2. After you have prepared a storyboard to your liking, carry it a step further and make up a dummy book.

BOOKS MENTIONED IN THIS CHAPTER
(IN ORDER OF APPEARANCE)

Snowflake Bentley, Jacqueline Briggs Martin, illustrated
    by Mary Azarian
Jumanji, Chris Van Allsburg
Joseph Had a Little Overcoat, Simms Taback
Kogi's Mysterious Journey, Elizabeth Partridge, illustrated
    by Aki Sogabe
Red Racer, Audrey Wood
Cock-a-Doodle-Do, Janet Stevens

OTHER ILLUSTRATORS
MENTIONED IN THIS CHAPTER
(IN ALPHABETICAL ORDER)

Jan Brett   Brian Pinkney
Eric Carle   Robert Quackenbush
Barbara Cooney   Maurice Sendak
Leo and Diane Dillon   Uri Shulevitz
Ezra Jack Keats   Peter Sis
Arnold Lobel   Vera Williams
Christopher Myers

18

Changing Markets

Finding the Right Publisher for Your Work

Book markets are constantly changing—expanding, contracting, reshaping. Within a year, the emphasis can shift from one kind of publishing to another or explode in ways we never expected. Anything that changes our lifestyles can trigger changes in the book industry.

FAT FUNDS

A major change in publishing occurred in the 1960s, when library budgets were fat with government funds. Books were published in great quantities and in lavish editions, because the money was there and people—mainly librarians—were buying them. An event of less media note was the introduction of mass market paperback reprints into the children's field. The only reprints available prior to that time were those produced by book clubs like Scholastic that had operated within the school system for years. With the advent of Dell's Yearling Books for Children, publishers began to release books from their backlist—books published over the years and still actively sold in hardcover. For the first time, you could buy children's books in paperback editions at a fraction of the hardcover cost. They began to make their way into bookstores and even libraries.

POP-UP BOOK GLUT

In the 1980s libraries, once responsible for 80 percent of the children's books purchased in the United States, were no longer the dependable buying source they had been due to cuts in federal funds. Publishers were forced to tap new markets for selling children's books, catering to the bookstore consumer rather than the institutional buyer. All of a sudden there was a glut of pop-up books, book-and-toy combinations, activity books, and books you could write in—lots of commercial properties that never worked in the library environment. The success of this shift accounted for an upsurge in children's book purchases and made up for the lost library market.

SERIES

There is nothing new about the popularity of series; many childhoods ago, stories about Nancy Drew and the Hardy Boys came on the scene and are still entertaining girls and boys. Series generally grow out of a demand by readers for more about certain characters, like J. K. Rowling's Harry Potter or the puppet people on Sesame Street, or on certain themes, as in R. L. Stine's Goosebumps series of horror stories or the Star Wars movies.

Each series has its own reason for being, and is almost always generated by marketing considerations. Ann M. Martin took on contemporary issues in her series, the Baby-Sitters Club, about a group of friends who start a baby-sitting service. Girls who baby-sit and are drawn to a group of friends who share common interests respond to the clearly plotted, realistically handled stories. Bonnie Bryant's Saddle Club series offers good characterizations and expert background on riding but more importantly, feeds into the adolescent girl's love of horses. My own string of books about Robert Dorfman started with one book (with no sequel in mind) about a boy who is not a super achiever but whose heart and intentions are good. A book club publisher saw the appeal in the character and asked for more.

HEALTHY INDUSTRY

The growth in independent children's bookstores as well as expansion of children's departments in major bookstores, reflected a healthy industry, and it wasn't all because of Harry Potter.

That phenomenon didn't hurt the statistics, but even before that a baby boom provided a new stream of readers and a huge population of well-educated young parents who believed that reading was key to their children's future success. Children's bookstores now account for about half of children's book sales.

ELECTRONICS EXPLOSION

Nothing affected the publishing industry more than the electronics explosion. Advanced computer technology in the methods of creating, researching, producing, and storing books had a profound effect on publishing, and that meant writers were affected, too. New markets appeared overnight online.

E-PUBLISHING

With the new technology, electronic publishing, or e-publishing, has become a reality. While the roots of creativity, the development of ideas, and the style in which you write are as important as ever, the method of producing books and delivering them to readers is in a constant state of change and will probably continue to be for years to come. This affects you as a writer by providing better and faster tools with which to write, more economical ways to research, accelerated production methods, faster communication with your editor, new markets for your books, more effective methods of advertising and selling your work, and more variety in how you may see your material published.

E-publishers have individual Web sites on which they display submissions guidelines. Follow these to submit work. Some publishers pay, although very little—not even as much as regular magazines, which at least offer copies of the magazine in payment. Others run contests, and if you win, you are paid a small amount. It's up to you whether it's worth it to have your work published in this way, and to see if any unexpected benefits arise from it. A bonus for one author who tried e-publishing was that a teacher in Japan wrote to ask permission to use one of her stories to help Japanese students learn to read English. Always be aware of the rights you are giving up when you publish your work this way; understand the publishing terms before agreeing to anything.

E-Books

E-books are simply books that are brought to readers digitally, to be read on the computer screen or by means of devices known as electronic readers. In other words, if an e-publisher publishes your book, rather than having it on paper, between covers, to keep on a book shelf, an e-book is available as an online download from the publisher, and you must have either "reading" software to display it on your computer screen, or some kind of handheld electronic device with which to read that book. It may never be printed on paper. Those who hold books sacred, and who think books must be words on paper pages bound by a cover, are having a hard time with the idea of e-books, but no one has predicted an end to paper books just because we have more electronic toys. Experts tell us that however technology enhances the way we entertain and inform ourselves, it will not replace the book as we know it.

The immediate practicality of e-books can be appreciated if you think of your days as a student when you lugged around a ton of textbooks that you only needed until the end of the term. An electronic reader can store hundreds of books at a time on a device no bigger than one paperback book. E-books would also make sense if you were traveling light, yet wanted to take along the top ten bestsellers to read on the deck of a yacht.

Advances in technology are inevitable. Think about reading an e-book and coming across a word you don't know. Perhaps there's a dictionary in your reader. Or perhaps it can even connect to the Internet for various links. Highlighting passages or lengthy revisions might be done with a simple click. Perhaps you can add animation to your text.

Of course there are flaws, as there are in any new ideas. The author Stephen King was enchanted by the prospect of publishing a book electronically and made headlines when he published his novel *Riding the Bullet* this way. It started off with great success, selling 400,000 copies on the first day alone, but within forty-eight hours, hackers had broken into the encrypted copy and it was all over the Internet.

Print-on-Demand

This is another offshoot of the electronics revolution, a method of printing books one copy at a time. What it means is that a library that wants to replace a well worn copy of a book can do so, even though the book is no longer available through traditional means. The publisher, rather than putting a book out of print and reverting rights to the author, can now keep a book technically in print forever, by just printing each one as customers demand it, rather than stockpiling books in costly warehousing facilities. Although the price per book may be higher, it serves the book buyer's purpose. On the down side, the writer may never get his rights back after a book stops selling in reasonable amounts, because a copy is always available, thus keeping him from reclaiming the rights and reissuing it with another company.

This has become a major contractual issue, and is best worked out clearly by you or your agent at the time of signing. For example, you will want a provision in the out-of-print clause that states your book cannot be considered "in print" if it is only available in print-on-demand format.

What Will They Think Of Next?

Some e-publishers want you to pay them a fee for putting your work online for editors to see, suggesting this might lead to your lucky break. What it mostly leads to is a flood of offers from subsidy publishers who will publish your book—any book, for that matter—for a price. It is a rare editor who looks for new writers this way.

By the time this book is printed, I will be wishing I could take advantage of another phenomenon, electronic ink, a way of constantly updating already published material, such as ads and guidebooks, to keep it up to date with the changes that seem to come into being daily.

What will they think of next and how will we know what's good for us? Learn by reading and by good examples. Ask for credentials and performance records. Get to know your way around so you can avoid disappointment.

RIDING THE WAVE

The impact of electronics on the publishing industry has already been astounding, and we can expect to see many new developments using digital technology, affecting everything from contracts and markets to how you work with an editor. We are still riding the wave of this new technology. Some day we may be exchanging e-books the way we do recipes. Since some predict that this change in how we do things is about as important as the invention of the printing press, we will have to keep ourselves informed. Here are a few sources to help you do just that—but beware—even they may change and you will have to find new ones to replace them!

LEARN THE MARKET WELL

Finding the right home for your work takes a great deal of skill—at least if you want to find it in your lifetime. With traditional publishers taking from four to eight months to respond to your submission, it makes sense that more writers are exploring online- and self-publishing. However, books as we know them, on paper and with covers, and the traditional channels that produce and distribute them, are still very much with us, and if all projections are correct, they will continue to be with us long into our future.

Learn your way around the shifting marketplace and keep abreast of it. Find out about trends and changes, and where and how editorial preferences and needs originate. Later, you can reevaluate your time and needs but, right now, nothing is more important to learn than this: if you want to sell your book, study the markets.

MARKETING GUIDES

Marketing guides note publishers that accept unsolicited manuscripts, as well as those who take multiple submissions. They note publishers that accept queries by e-mail, and offer the submissions procedures of various publishing houses. There are a few standard sources of general market news that are useful, reliable, and up to date (see appendix V for more about this and other marketing information).

Writers' Magazines

Among the most popular magazines for writers are *The Writer*, *Writer's Digest*, and *Poets & Writers Magazine*. While not specifically directed to children's book writers, they have articles of general interest to all writers and marketing reports with the most up-to-date information on changes and trends. Occasionally, they publish something specifically for children's writers.

Magazines just for children's writers exist, mostly through subscriptions. They offer market news and/or strategies for success, and all offer support for the working writer. *Children's Writer*, published originally for students of the Institute of Children's Literature, is now available to the public, and is one of the most thorough and helpful publications, with articles, marketing analysis, news, and tips for writers. Others include *The Society of Children's Book Writers and Illustrators Bulletin*, a bimonthly publication for members of that organization; and *Children's Book Insider*, a monthly newsletter with articles and market news.

An advantage to keeping your eyes and ears open to general industry news is that you may find a second market for some of your work. Perhaps the research you did for your book on tropical rain forests left you with overflowing, unused files packed with interesting information. In your readings, you may discover that a new children's magazine has been started, featuring environmental issues. The editor might just be interested in an article about the wildlife that lives in the forest canopies, and how their existence is threatened if we do not preserve the rain forests. You may also find that other publications need fillers—anecdotes, odd and interesting facts, humor, puzzles—and you may be able to put together some bits and pieces for them from your files.

Writers' Annuals

Each year, *Writer's Digest* publishes a thick hardcover volume, *Children's Writer's & Illustrator's Market*, containing articles, reference material, market lists, publishers' addresses, submission requirements, and other related information for the active writer. It is available at bookstores. If you are at the submitting stage of writing, it would be wise to buy the latest edition, to keep up with the changes in publishers' staffs and needs. Browse through it for marketing information as well as general helpful suggestions and articles on related topics, contributed by major people in children's publishing.

Trade Journals

The weekly publication of and about the publishing trade is *Publishers Weekly*, which also has an online edition. This magazine keeps you current with news of the publishing industry as it relates to the bookseller. It devotes a page every week to reviews of new children's books for the bookstore buyer. Two issues a year, in February and July, are devoted to children's publishing and include previews of forthcoming spring and fall books, plus additional articles and features.

Another online magazine, *Publishers Lunch*, is an informative digest of publishing news that comes to you daily, if you subscribe, and it's free.

School Library Journal and the American Library Association's *Booklist*, are also helpful. The reviews in these publications give the writer some idea of how a book is judged by the library profession, a major purchaser of children's books.

You will be amazed at how much background information you can and will pick up in these articles and reviews. Perhaps you will learn how editors decide what their publishing needs are and how they find authors or make difficult choices when buying manuscripts, or what makes a library buyer turn down a nonfiction book by a well-known author.

The previews of forthcoming books in *Publishers Weekly* may indicate that a publisher is starting a new series of books, or that a new small publisher is emerging. This is worth noting; they may be looking for new writers with new projects. Although their budgets may be smaller and distribution capabilities limited, a small press can offer you more personalized attention than a large publisher.

Writers' Organizations

Although many organizations for writers insist that writers be published as a requirement for joining, others are more liberal and even encourage beginning writers with information and services to help them get started. One is especially important to children's writers: The Society of Children's Book Writers and Illustrators (SCBWI), an international organization devoted solely to the interests of writers and illustrators of children's books. The SCBWI offers a newsletter to its members providing publishing news and marketing information, announcements of important events and legislation related to their members, as well as articles about craft. Regional advisors sponsor meetings, conferences, workshops, and critique groups for its members, some of which are open to nonmembers as well. Attending one or more of these events can be not only inspiring but, on a practical level, can put you in closer touch with editors who may be looking for your kind of book or style. Talking to other writers, too, can lead to interesting information and possible work. You might consider joining such a group in order to keep up with news and to take advantage of the social contacts and services offered (see appendix VII for information about this and other organizations).

The Author's Guild is a society of published authors advocating free speech, fair compensation, and copyright protection. Members can take contracts to them to review. If you are not yet published, you may join as an associate member (http://www.authorsguild.org).

PEN, known primarily for its defense of free expression around the world, is another organization worth knowing (http://www.pen.org).

Guidelines

These are available in print and online from publishers, particularly for specific lines of books. They give you clear information on what material to submit and how, what you will be paid, manuscript length, and other details. When you send for guidelines, remember to enclose a self-addressed stamped envelope. Guidelines can be informative and sometimes even amusing.

Where else would you learn that in some teen romance series teenagers—even those who are madly in love with each other—may touch, but only from the waist up!

Networking

Knowing the sources of information is a large part of keeping up with your business, but it isn't the only part. You have to go out and get information or make contacts when you have a lead. Only then will you get the word on the latest writing assignments and opportunities open to beginners.

Here are several scenarios in which you might find yourself. You read, in the "Marketplace" section of *Children's Writer,* that a publishing house that publishes only nonfiction is seeking biographies for young readers. You have been following the career of a bright young star, a woman who has made important discoveries in the search for a cure for cancer, and you would love to research and write her biography. The publisher wants your resume with clips (any clippings from newspapers or magazines in which your work appeared) or writing samples. You have no clips but you immediately send your proposal for a biography of the scientist, explaining why you think she would make a good subject and why you are the person to write this book, along with your resume and a sample of your writing.

As you browse through the latest copy of the *Bulletin,* which you receive bimonthly as a member of the Society of Children's Book Writers and Illustrators, you find that an editor who has been with one publishing house for eight years has gone to another house to expand their children's list, especially its picture book line. During a recent writing class, your instructor told you the picture book you had been working on is ready to submit to a publisher. You check it out and learn you don't even need a query letter. Before twenty-four hours have gone by, you have mailed your manuscript, freshly printed, to the editor at her new publishing house.

In the section "At Presstime" in *Children's Book Insider,* you read that a publishing company is looking for plays for the school market. You have written a play for young children which has been sitting on the shelf because you didn't know what to do with it. You dust if off, reread it, make revisions, and query that publisher, all within days of reading the notice.

After a writers' conference, you are talking with other writers and discover that there is a new monthly magazine that features history for young people in an interesting format. History is your special interest. You have not yet published a book, but you feel you can successfully write an article. You send for a copy of the magazine and request a copy of their guidelines and theme list for the coming year.

Talking with a writer friend, you learn that the various teenage romance lines publish strict guidelines for their authors. Young adult books are your area of interest, so you write to the editors of each of these lines asking for a copy of their guidelines.

In a previews issue of *Publishers Weekly* that you read at the library, you learn that a publishing house is going to issue a series in the next year on water sports. You would love to combine your interest in kite-surfing with your interest in writing, so you query the editor, saying that you would like to discuss some ideas for this series with him.

Incidentally, you pay your own research expenses, so don't let your ideas get too exotic. It is true, however, that you may be able to take these expenses as tax deductions if you are a working writer; something to discuss with your tax accountant.

None of the above situations is farfetched. Some of them, in fact, are real, based on situations I have witnessed. As in all businesses there is a lot of competition, and what you do with what you've got is closely related to your success. Brushing aside valuable information is a little like saying "No, thank you" to the offer of a free ticket when you're standing on line at the box office in the rain. Leads like this take some of the pain and frustration out of getting a foot in the door and sometimes are the very thing you need to get started.

THE NET

The Internet has been known to bring people together in more ways than one. For writers, it's the best thing to come along since windshield wipers. It's fine for research, keeping up with publishing news, chatting with other writers, and seeing a publisher's catalog online, but it's also a great resource for marketing information. Appendix V lists various Web sites to check out where children's book markets are available at the click of a mouse.

SUGGESTIONS—CHAPTER 18

1. Find five publishers to whom you would submit a contemporary novel about Phil, a high school junior who holds five different jobs after school—all with funny results—to pay for a Mustang he wants to buy when he gets his driver's license.
2. You have a mystery novel about the theft of money collected by a class of third-graders to buy uniforms for the soccer team and what they do to find the thief. Would you submit it to Chelsea House Publishers? Justify your answer.

SOURCES OF INFORMATION MENTIONED IN THIS CHAPTER (IN ORDER OF APPEARANCE)

The Writer
Writer's Digest
Poets & Writers Magazine
Children's Writer
The Society of Children's Book Writers and Illustrators Bulletin
Children's Book Insider
Children's Writer's & Illustrator's Market
Publishers Weekly
Publishers Weekly Online http://www.publishersweekly.com
Publishers Lunch http://www.publisherslunch.com
School Library Journal
American Library Association *Booklist*
Society of Children's Book Writers and Illustrators
The Author's Guild
PEN

PART FIVE

A Publisher
in Your Future

Good stories are not written. They are rewritten. . . .
    —Phyllis A. Whitney, *Writing Juvenile
    Stories and Novels*

19

Out of the Slush Pile and into the Fire

What Publishers Do

What happens at the other end, where your manuscript is received? Is it handled with care? Is it read by anybody?

Publishers have the right not to read unsolicited manuscripts (those sent directly by the author to the publisher without being requested), but will generally let it be known if this is their policy. In those houses where manuscripts from the general public are welcome, a staff member generally sorts the mail each day as it comes in, putting unsolicited manuscripts in one pile, known by the awful term *slush pile,* and those from agents or requested by the editor, in another. This staff member keeps a record, or log, of all manuscripts received each day. An acknowledgment is not usually sent to the author. If you want to receive one, enclose your own stamped self-addressed postcard to be checked off and mailed back to you. This is not a guarantee that it will be sent, but most houses comply.

READERS' REPORTS

The manuscript is then given to a first reader. This may be someone on the staff or a freelancer with professional qualifications. All manuscripts are looked at carefully. Those that are poorly written or badly imitative will probably not get a full reading. Neither will a manuscript totally inappropriate for that publisher, or sloppily prepared. No editorial staff will waste its time on something that is hopeless or a strain to read. However, professional readers know what to look for. If the first few pages of a novel do not work, a reader knows enough to skip ahead and read another few pages, and perhaps another few, to see if things improve. This can happen in novels, especially first novels.

The size of the manuscript is no indication of how quickly it will be read. Technically, the four-page picture book script that came in after the twenty thick novels should be read after the novels, but I remember, when I was an editor, wanting to break up the longer readings with short pieces, and therefore reading some out of order. For the most part, however, your manuscript takes its place in the order received. Manuscripts sent in by agents may be read first. The reason for the privilege is that the agent has already read the work and deemed it publishable, which is similar to what a first reader does. This carries a lot of weight if the agent has a good reputation. Agents who do not do their homework and send out manuscripts unread or not ready for publication find that the practice immediately backfires and their manuscripts are back in the slush pile.

If the reader says that a manuscript is not acceptable, it is sent back to the author, usually with a simple form letter. If a manuscript has possibilities, a written report is made up, including a brief summary of the plot and an evaluation. If the report is favorable, the manuscript will end up on the editor's desk. If she likes it and wants to buy it, she brings it before an editorial or acquisitions committee, and makes a pitch for it. This is where the final decision is made. Few editors have the authority to acquire manuscripts on their own.

EDITORIAL COMMENTS

Consider the editor's point of view; she cannot buy every good manuscript she sees, but must constantly strive for variety in subject matter, style, and age group. Maybe your next story will be better suited to her needs.

If she takes the time to add personal comments, note the editor's name and send more work to her. If you get a letter suggesting revisions, consider her advice. If you disagree with the editor's ideas, move on to the next publisher, but if her suggestions seem valid, make the revisions, and send the manuscript back to her for a rereading before sending it to any other publisher.

Multiple Revisions

If an editor asks for a second revision, with no offer of a contract, you will have to decide whether the suggestions made are worth your time and consideration. Are they made for a better book or to suit that particular editor's personal taste? If they are the latter, and there is no offer of a contract, it may not be advisable to go ahead with more changes; another editor may feel differently about what is needed. If the advice is helpful and there is no question that the suggestions would improve the book, do what the editor asks. If she suggests a third revision, you have the right to ask the editor's intent, and talk about a contract.

A publisher will rarely make a commitment to a beginning writer for anything but a finished work of fiction or a fully detailed proposal with sample chapters for a nonfiction idea. It is possible to send a partial manuscript of a novel with the remainder summarized; a publisher will not offer you a contract, but she may let you know if she is seriously interested in the project.

Rejections

There are many manuscripts that show promise but are not bought, simply because the publisher's list isn't big enough to accommodate them, or because the work that needs to be done with the author is more than the editor's time will allow. Sometimes a perfectly good manuscript is rejected because it does not stand out in any way—it has no special quality. It takes a good bit of self-confidence and good critical sense to overcome the feeling of personal rejection that comes with returned manuscripts, but if you can understand decisions from the editor's point of view, you can get through rejections a lot more easily.

Many writers wish editors would say why their stories are rejected. The fact is publishing is a business, not a school. Editors and readers read your work for the sole purpose of finding and selecting good publishable material so they can produce books, sell them, and make a profit for their company. They expect the work that comes to them to be of professional quality and that any help you need will have been sought before you submit your work. More than half of all unsolicited manuscripts received by publishers are poorly written or submitted without regard to already existing books or the publishers' interests. This is why some publishers have closed their doors to unsolicited works: the percentage of publishable manuscripts discovered in the slush pile does not warrant the expense of looking for them.

CONTRACT

When a contract is offered, it is usually done by letter, or by phone with a letter to follow. An editor may want to talk with you first, to discuss the work to be done on the manuscript. Once the editor knows how you feel about the work to be done and what it will be like to work with you, she may offer you a contract. You will be given time to look over the contract. If you have an agent, the first contact will be made between the editor and your agent, and your agent will inform you of the sale. Once the basic terms have been discussed by those two parties, you will talk to and work with the editor yourself.

There are different kinds of contracts. A "work-for-hire" contract is one that pays a flat fee with no provision for further payments or royalties. In work-for-hire contracts, you usually agree to give up all rights to the work and the publishing house copyrights the work in its name. Read your contract carefully to know which rights you are signing away.

Royalty contracts are standardized in form with terms, such as advance and royalty rate, to be filled in. Advances vary according to the experience of the author and how many copies of the book the publishing house figures it can sell. Royalties seldom vary; 10 percent is the standard share allotted for author and illustrator combined. For a nonillustrated book, such as a teenage novel, you would receive the full 10 percent. For a picture book, where the illustrator is equally important to the book, you would probably share the royalty evenly.

As you publish more books, your advances will probably increase, and sometimes your royalty rate will go up. Relatively few writers earn more than a 10 percent share, but that doesn't mean you shouldn't be protected. There should, ideally, be an escalation clause in your contract which states that if your book sells more than a certain number of copies, your royalty will increase. If there isn't such a clause, try to get one included.

Some companies have a clause stating that royalties will be based on net proceeds rather than gross. A book selling for $12.95 would earn you $1.295 per book on a gross system. On a net system, various publishers' discounts would be included before the royalty is figured, so if a purchaser gets a 40 percent discount, your royalty becomes $1.295 less 40 percent, or $.777 per copy. Publishers who base royalties on net proceeds do, in some cases, offer higher royalty rates to compensate. You can see how this would seriously affect your income, so understand the contract you sign, note the terms carefully, and avoid surprises later. You can always turn down an offer if a contract seems unfair and the publisher is unwilling to negotiate. Agents are extremely helpful here, because they know what the negotiable points are and how far they can push.

The option clause, giving the publisher the right to your next work, is standard for a first book. On your next contract, you can negotiate to remove this clause so that you are free to submit your next book to anyone you please, or at least be more specific about the nature of the work covered by the clause. For example, if your first book is a picture book, your second contract might describe your option as a "work of a similar nature," so that it is only a picture book manuscript that is covered by your option clause. Or it may be spelled out more specifically, naming the type of book, age group, and whether it is to be fiction or nonfiction.

EARNINGS

There is no way to guess how much money you can make on a book. A lot depends on the state of book budgets in libraries, the health of retail bookstores, reviews, promotion and publicity, subsidiary rights sales, and plain good luck. An unfavorable review in *School Library Journal* may curtail the sales of a book that leans heavily on the library market. On the other hand, a plug on TV may cause a spike in sales in bookstores. When, years ago, Johnny Carson read excerpts from my book *You Can't Eat Peanuts in Church and Other Little-Known Laws* on the *Tonight Show*, sales jumped sky-high.

If everything goes perfectly, you might receive an advance of, let's say, $10,000 (for the sake of easier math) from a hardcover publisher for your first novel. If your book has a catalog price of $16.00 (again for easy math), your royalty (10 percent) will give you $1.60 for each copy sold. If you sell 2,000 copies in the first year after publication, that will be a total of $3,200. No taxes have been withheld. Subtract this amount from your $10,000 advance and, in about one year, you have earned back only about a third of your advance. You must earn another $6,800 before you will see any more income from that book. In some cases, the advance is all you will ever see for a book; it may even go out of print before you have earned back the rest. If this happens, your contract probably protects you from having to pay back the remainder of the advance, but it is something to consider when drawing up a contract.

In your second year, perhaps you sell 1,500 copies of the book. That's another $2,400 for you, but you won't see it; it will be deducted from the balance you owe, leaving you with $4,400 left to earn. But don't despair! Perhaps you will sell the paperback reprint rights for $7,500, giving you an additional $3,750, after the fee is split fifty-fifty with the publisher. Perhaps in your next royalty period you will earn enough money to actually receive a check.

A large amount of money sounds good at first, but consider that everything you earn on this book comes over a period of two or three or even more years. You would need quite a lot of books in print to bring in a reasonable income. And, if you sell a book that requires illustrations, you will have to share earnings with the illustrator.

The fact of the matter is, for most people, writing children's books is not a lucrative business, but there are some writers who earn their living at it. It is the kind of field in which you have to weigh the rewards of the work against the risks and struggle. Certainly, you should not consider giving up a full-time paying job at this point to stay at home and do nothing but write children's books . . . not if you have rent to pay and food to buy. If you stay with it, and find your success, you will know when the time has come to give up the other job.

SUBSIDIARY RIGHTS

Subsidiary rights to your work are all offshoots of your creation. They include paperback rights, book club rights, movie and TV rights, toys and games based on characters you have created, and so forth. Publishers are automatically entitled to book rights only, including paperback and book club, within the United States and its territories. Anything else must be negotiated with you. Your agent, if you have one, will try to sell foreign rights, movie rights, and whatever else is feasible. In the absence of an agent, the publisher will act as your agent and help you to sell those rights.

If Five Star Movie Productions wants to buy the movie rights to your novel *Teen Dreams,* they will go to your publisher. The publisher will direct the movie company to your agent or, if you have no agent, talk to the movie people on your behalf, consulting with you about the terms.

If a paperback publisher wants to buy reprint rights to your book, the hardcover publisher can negotiate the rights without your consent, because they are still book rights. You may be consulted about terms, but the disposition of those rights is up to the publisher. If there is an agent involved on this book, she will still receive her commission, for your part of the income on this deal.

When the time comes, read through your contract carefully; it isn't as "Greek" as you think. With the help of one or more of the publications listed in appendix IV and a little effort, you can understand the various clauses so that you will know what you are talking about. A little knowledge goes a very long way. If necessary, hire a lawyer to help you understand your contract.

Vanity Publishing

If you simply want to show off a book with your name on it, you can hire any vanity press to print and bind whatever you give them. These companies exist solely to take advantage of the ego and vulnerability of writers who cannot get their work published through normal channels and who feel a bound book gives them validity as writers. It doesn't. A vanity press will publish anything for a price.

Subsidy Publishers

Subsidy publishers are a bit different and can sometimes be helpful, offering various services to the writer who may have good reason for going off on his own to publish a book. Technically, they can assist with any or all stages of publishing your book, from the editorial process through the production and promotion of your work.

For a fee, paid by you, they will print and bind your manuscript and deliver 5,000 copies (or some other prearranged number) to your door. Does that mean your book is now published? Not really. Publishing is much more than printing and binding. Who will review your book? Many books will not be purchased without reviews by professionals to guide the purchasers. Who will distribute it? Those 5,000 copies will do you no good sitting in your garage. And who will buy your book? Maybe you can sell fifty copies to friends and relatives; then what? You have to let people know that your book exists, so you will have to advertise.

The wrinkle here is subsidy publishers' poor reputation, earned over many years of preying on new writers, of promising services and results they did not deliver. These publishers can appear to be agents, or editors who simply want to read your work for possible publication, and after they read it, give it high praise, saying they would like to publish it. There is nothing illegitimate in this process. Hopeful new writers are only too willing to hear that someone likes their work and they succumb to the attraction of a contract, an editor, and the promise of seeing their book published. Somewhere along the line, you are asked to pay the costs of publishing your book, and even when you pay (usually thousands of dollars) for having your manuscript "published," the company may or may not provide all the necessary services, or may provide them scantily. You may suddenly find that you are responsible for finding and hiring an illustrator, or for distributing the books once they are printed. Otherwise you may end up with 5,000 copies of your book and no way to sell them, short of loading up a wheelbarrow and knocking on every door up and down the street. Few bookstores will sell books published this way.

Subsidy publishers can be helpful, however, if they detail the various services they offer, specify what you can expect from each, and how much it costs. Ideally they will tell you honestly how much you will have to be involved in any of these stages, and what they cannot or will not do.

How do you know if one of these publishers is right for you? Knowledge will go a long way, so ask questions. Ask for the credentials of the company—who owns it, who runs it, how long they have been in business. Ask for the names of other clients, so you can speak to them. Ask to see their published books. Ask to see one of their contracts. See if they are listed in the members' list of the Children's Book Council or on the publishers' list of the Society of Children's Book Writers and Illustrators. (Once you are a member of this organization, you can get this and other helpful literature at no cost.) Both organizations are listed in appendix VII. Hire a lawyer to read everything before you sign it, and then, just for good luck, spit in your hands, turn around three times, and make a wish.

Self-Publishing

Self-publishing is not a new idea, but technology has brought it to a respectable new place in a writer's life. With easily obtainable software programs, it is a viable route to publishing a work in an affordable way for a limited audience. It gives individuals the tools to write, design, illustrate, and publish their own books with the help of various software programs and a professional print shop to print and bind your book. I publish several books on my own, for fun, using the software that came with my Macintosh computer, and a reliable Hewlett Packard inkjet printer. I bind them with a spiral binding machine that sits on my file cabinet. The books I publish are for myself or for students of my workshops, including a cookbook to which many of them contributed recipes and several workbooks based on my teaching exercises, which you can find listed in appendix VIII. This is self-publishing at its most modest, but it serves my purpose.

Barbara Comfort had a more ambitious project in mind when she tried to sell mysteries set in her small town of Landgrove, Vermont, to big city publishers who were not interested in the local color. Comfort had a small local press print a trunkload of copies of her first book, *Vermont Village Murder*, and began selling them out of her car to bookstores in southern Vermont. She sold enough of her books to draw a local following, and eventually attracted a publisher as well, who published her next books. This was one author's way of investing in herself, and her hard work paid off.

There have been some success stories with self-publishing and, after all, some of the most famous writers—Virginia Woolf, D. H. Lawrence, Henry Thoreau—published some of their own works, but look into the practice thoughtfully before you consider it for yourself. It may be right for your cherished book of poems or your family history, which may have only a small audience, but if you want your book to reach a wide readership, it is usually wiser to follow the traditional procedures and find ways to be creative in your writing instead of in your publishing.

I have not met anyone yet who has had the success they had anticipated with a self-published children's book, but I accept the reality that it could happen. At least if you are doing it yourself, you know exactly what you can and can't do and what it will cost, and you will have control over the entire project.

SUGGESTIONS—CHAPTER 19

1. You are a first reader for Children's Delight Publishing Company. Write a reader's report on the picture book text for *Where the Wild Things Are* as though it were being submitted as new material today.

2. You are an editor. A manuscript comes to you for a novel that is well written but badly developed. Draft a letter to the author to accompany the returned manuscript.

3. You are an editor. You receive a very promising first novel. You hate to lose this promising new writer, but you have all

the novels you can publish for the next two years. Draft a letter to the author to accompany the returned manuscript.

BOOKS MENTIONED IN THIS CHAPTER
(IN ORDER OF APPEARANCE)

You Can't Eat Peanuts in Church and Other Little-Known Laws, Barbara Seuling (out-of-print)
Vermont Village Murder, Barbara Comfort
Where the Wild Things Are, Maurice Sendak

20

Your Editor—Friend or Dragon?

Working with an Editor

Manuscripts are bought in a state considered "publishable," but often revision and polishing follow to squeeze out the best the author can do for the finest book that can be. A good editor is vital in this process.

An editor is trained to observe and will see many things that you cannot see when you are so close to your material. It can be as simple as pointing out that your heroine behaves more like a teenager than a ten-year-old, or it can be more complex, like seeing that you tend to withdraw from potentially strong scenes rather than confront the emotional issues involved. Good editors do not rewrite your material; they guide you, making suggestions, opening your eyes to new possibilities, and discussing solutions with you, but they leave the writing—and all final decisions about content—to you.

BE FLEXIBLE

If you disagree with an editor, and there is no satisfactory compromise, you will almost always be allowed to win your point, within reason. Be flexible and listen to what the editor is saying. You may find, after all, that there is something there. A writer will listen and bend, if necessary, even at the expense of a certain favorite phrase or passage in the manuscript, if the advice is sound and the book would be improved by the change. An editor usually knows how to point things out so that the author can comfortably accept the change.

I once submitted a picture book manuscript consisting of four little stories about two animal friends. The editor liked it, bought it, and proceeded to edit it. We had several discussions, usually about the behavior of the animals and the logistics of details. Several improvements came out of these talks. Then, quite suddenly, she made a suggestion that left me gasping.

"I think you ought to drop the first story," she said.

"How can I drop it?" I cried. "That's the story that sets up the relationship between the two friends."

"Exactly," replied my editor. "You set them up for a friendship that is perfectly clear from their actions. You don't need to explain it. The first story slows it down. The second story starts right in, and it's obvious that they are friends. Look at it and think about it. Let me know what you decide."

Needless to say, it was devastating to consider cutting out one-fourth of my book. I was attached to that story. In the next few days, going over it again and again, I saw that my editor was right. I have had cause many times since to admire her judgment. The book, *The Great Big Elephant and the Very Small Elephant,* was published in hardcover, received good reviews, and was subsequently purchased by two book clubs, in hard- and softcover, and by a book club in England. No one ever missed that first story.

When Your Editor Leaves

It can happen that an editor you have been working with suddenly leaves the company—right in the middle of your book. What do you do? Some writers become so attached to their editors that they follow them wherever they go, contract permitting. If it does not, you must finish out your contract with the present company and perhaps when you sign up your next work it can be with your original editor at her new company. Or you may decide that it is worth staying at the present publishing house, even without the editor you liked, because you want the continuity of working with one house. However you deal with it, losing an editor is an unsettling experience and it takes a while to get over it.

Author/editor relationships can be satisfying, challenging, and productive but, alas, they can also be otherwise. I have known authors who worked with editors who clearly hated their work, and others who never spoke to their editors—just received letters outlining what needed to be done, did the revisions without a murmur, and sent the manuscript back, never to hear another word until the finished book arrived in the mail. If you are stuck with an editor you don't like, there is very little to be done about it, except look forward to taking your next manuscript elsewhere. Even if you have an option clause that requires you to submit your next work to the same publisher, you are entitled to terms that are satisfactory; if they are not, you can take it to another house.

In Production

You may be asked to transmit your final manuscript to your publisher electronically. When the editing process is completed, all corrections are made to the file and a CD is burned. The printer makes a plate from the CD which is put on the press and voilà! The technical jargon for this is CTP, or computer to plate.

There comes a time, after the final revision, after you and your editor have completed the editorial phase of the book, when months may go by without a word from your publisher. You will imagine all sorts of terrible things: your book has been postponed indefinitely; your manuscript was eaten by the editor's dog; your publishing house has gone bankrupt; they have decided to drop you and have not been able to tell you so. The truth is, the editor and the whole publishing house staff are working on dozens of other books while yours is off in the copyediting, production, or design department. Each department has the manuscript for a period of time before it is passed on to someone else, until it has gone through all the stages preparatory to publishing.

Page Proofs

You will see the copyedited manuscript with queries to be addressed, and you will see page proofs. You can still make some corrections at this point. A second and even a third set of pages may follow, with final design elements in place, such as page numbers and artwork. The further along you are, the more costly it is to make any but the most necessary corrections, so these are for one last tweaking, not serious revision. You may see an artist's sketch for the book jacket, and flap copy or catalog copy, but other than that, nothing much happens on your end until you see your finished book, with your name printed boldly on the front and spine.

The process, from signing the contract to autographing your first copy for your mother, averages about one year. Waiting for an illustrator's schedule to open up to work on your book may push that to two years, even three. On the other hand, books in series may be produced on a faster schedule to keep up with buyer demand.

In any case, you will have to learn patience as a writer or, at the very least, what to do while you're waiting. Don't sit back and do nothing. Talk about your upcoming books with your local booksellers and set up book signings for its publication date. Make school visits and read or talk about your book to children. They will love being privy to a book that is not yet in the bookstores, from the author's own experience.

Talk to your publisher's publicity director about what you can do to help promote your book. Offer to talk to children in classrooms online about your book when it comes out; this would need time to be set up. Discuss your next book with your editor; thinking about a new book takes some of the anxiety out of waiting for the present one to come out. Be active in your own career as much as possible.

Your chances for subsequent publication have improved considerably with this first success, and you need to feed success to keep it alive. So, get to work! You are a professional writer now.

SUGGESTIONS—CHAPTER 20

Spend some time getting your tools in order.

1. Buy a dozen each of 7 by 9 and 9 by 12-inch envelopes.
2. Self-address half of the envelopes so they are handy when you are ready to mail a manuscript.
3. Buy a small postage scale and an assortment of stamps to save you many trips to and waiting in line at the post office.
4. Buy a waterproof marker for addressing large envelopes so that the address is clear and easy to read.

21

Joining the Writing Community

Taking an Active Role

The one ingredient lacking, so far, is contact with other writers on a regular basis. People with office jobs have a kind of extended family at the office, friendships are made, support is offered, and information is shared.

It is important for writers to have such relationships with their colleagues, but we have to go about establishing them differently, since we write mostly in isolation.

One children's writer, Audrey Baird, had exactly the right instinct when she started a magazine for children's writers and illustrators called *Once Upon a Time* . . . She doesn't offer marketing advice, which so many others do, but simply provides a kind of gathering place—"like meeting over the back yard fence," she says—for writers and illustrators who need the support and encouragement of other writers going through the same struggles. Professional people from all areas of children's publishing provide regular columns of support and advice.

In the midwest, the Children's Literature Network was organized under Vicki Palmquist to connect those who are involved with children and their reading in one way or another: authors, illustrators, editors, publishers, reading teachers, librarians, media specialists, booksellers, and book reviewers. Although there is a "members only" section of their Web site (http://www .childrensliteraturenetwork.org) much of it is open to the public and provides a wide variety of information and advice.

Some writers form local groups that meet on a regular basis. They talk about their work, about their experiences with publishers, and they may even exchange manuscripts. Other groups meet to read works in progress for support and criticism. If members are spread out and must travel a good distance to attend a meeting, it can be quite a social event. One group of New England writers meets on a bimonthly basis. Each meeting starts with a potluck dinner. Afterward, book news is shared among the members—new contracts, published books, reviews, author tours, work problems, and so on. The rest is purely social but inevitably focuses on books, editors, and related topics. For some members it is the only completely free day, away from family and other obligations, in which they can indulge in the total pleasure of being a writer among other writers.

A small group in New York functions more as a support group than a social or critique group. Members share information about jobs and help each other over the rough spots. Still other groups invite professional people such as editors, writers, illustrators, and agents to come and talk, chipping in to pay for the visitor's honorarium.

Some years ago, a writers' group I belonged to in New York was the catalyst for a book project, although that was not its original intent. The city's libraries were in crisis, and at one of our meetings we came up with an idea about how we could help, and *The New York Kid's Book* was born. We were all unknown writers at the time, but we solicited voluntary contributions from other writers and artists, some literary stars among them, edited it all, and found a publisher who was willing to go along with our plan—donating the royalties to the hurting libraries.

Online critique groups have sprung up following classes and workshops, where writers wanted to remain together as friends and colleagues. However you use your group, it is important because it puts you together with other writers so that you become more informed and get away from the isolated writer's existence now and then.

To start a writers' group, talk to someone at your local library; perhaps you can put up a notice there to attract other writers in the area. Advertise in your local paper or post notices on university or community bulletin boards. Once you find interested people, arrange a location for the first meeting (schools, libraries, or churches are good places to start) and set a date.

Your first meeting will tell you in which direction you want to go, whether the members want to read manuscripts or talk shop, or whether you will deal actively with issues close to writers' hearts.

We have already talked about the activities of the Society of Children's Book Writers and Illustrators and various other workshops and conferences (see chapter 7). Through your contacts with other writers, you will have a deeper understanding of the writing business and, at the same time, feel a part of a community, which is excellent for the spirit. I have seen it happen over and over again, one writer sharing an important piece of information with another, or one writer introducing another to someone with similar interests.

Book Talks

Once you have a book published, there are other ways to meet people who have an interest in children's books, particularly yours. Make arrangements with your local public schools or libraries to set up book talks with children. Consider these a service to your community, during which you practice the art of the book talk until you can take your presentation farther afield. Publishers often need authors who are willing to travel to various schools around the country, for book fairs and author and illustrator festivals. Teachers who work with children on writing love to have real live authors come in and talk to the children about the writing process. Once you have a good presentation worked out and understand the interchange between the writer and the children, you may want to charge a fee for your talks. Since this is part of being a writer, you need not feel awkward about being paid for such jobs; you must give up writing time to do the talks and to travel. It is only when you are learning (practicing) that you do it for nothing, or when the organization for which you do it is special to you and you do it as a favor. Publishers will help you set up book talks and take care of arranging transportation, delivery of books to sell at fairs, and other conveniences.

Promote your book in any way that you can. Fill out the questionnaire that is sent to you by your publisher's promotion department; make it interesting and lively. It is important in matching you up with requests for speaking engagements.

Keep in touch with your publisher before and after publication of your book through your editor or the publicity department. Let them know that you would like to be involved and that you are willing to speak, grant interviews, attend autographings, appear at bookstores to help celebrate National Children's Book Week, Dr. Seuss's birthday, Halloween, or some other special event.

In preparation for all of this, remember to save your assorted notes, rough drafts, scraps, galleys, and any material related to the creation and production of your book. Ask the publisher to return your manuscript when she no longer needs it; an edited manuscript is always interesting to a young audience. Character sketches and anything that shows how your ideas evolved and developed are also fascinating. In some of my school visits, I took my brother along, who was the prototype for the character of Mr. Dorfman in my Robert books. The kids love meeting the model for a character!

BOOK PROMOTION

Your book will be promoted in various standard ways, and perhaps some new ones. It will appear in the publisher's catalog, which comes out long before the book is off the press. This catalog is sent to libraries and bookstores across the country and is given to the publisher's salespeople, who visit book buyers carrying sample books, pages, pictures, jackets, and catalogs.

Twice a year the editors address the sales force directly to speak on behalf of their books. The editor tries to give the salespeople highlights on each book and essential information that will help in the sales representative's brief bookstore presentation. On the road, salespeople refresh themselves on the individual books by means of an information sheet, prepared by the editors. These sheets give vital information about the book and the author.

Your book is also announced in certain trade journals, which are read by important book purchasers, and shown online at the publisher's Web site, as well as those of the major online bookstores. Keep yourself informed and ask your editor questions whenever you can. If there is a house-generated publication that is sent to libraries, ask about it and how you can see that your book is mentioned in it. Inquire about whether you can help in any way.

Books are often bought by school and public librarians on the basis of a few dependable sources of reviews, since most institutions cannot examine all the available books before purchase. If a book gets poor reviews in all of these, it will not be purchased by libraries. If two out of four don't like it, it has a limited chance. If only one doesn't like it, the damage is slight. All editors look for favorable reviews in all four, of course, for guaranteed sales. (See appendix II for a list of major reviewers.)

Some library systems have book examination centers, but smaller libraries have to depend on reviews, catalogs, salespeople, or jobbers, which are companies that buy large quantities of books from all publishers and sell them to the libraries at a discount, giving the libraries one place to order from instead of dozens.

When you are talking to your editor before your book goes to press, ask if they are going to run any bookmarks or promotion pieces with your book. These can be inserted on the press sheet on which your book is printed, which is economical for the publisher. Bookmarks are useful when doing book talks. The children love it when you can leave them with some "souvenir" of your visit.

Haunt your local bookshop and ask for your book. If it is not there, ask why it isn't, and try to get the store to order it. Do this in as pleasant a manner as possible; offer to do a book signing. You want to remain on good terms with your local bookstore.

Do everything you can to get your book noticed and do it as soon as the book comes out, or even before. After a few months, your publisher will not spend time helping you to promote your book, not because of ill intent, but because new books that are coming out demand her attention. You will be pretty much on your own, except for the occasional book talk that the publisher may help you set up.

SELF-PROMOTION

Instead of pouting when your turn is over, have a plan ready for self-promotion. Write up a piece about your book for the local newspaper. Use the telephone, newspapers, radio, and TV to help get your book and what you do across to the public. Create a Web page and link it to other children's book Web sites. You owe it to yourself and your book, and your publisher will be happy to work with you if you are self-sufficient in this way.

START SOMETHING

Now that you have come to the end of this book, don't stop, whatever you do. Get involved in the business of publishing and the joy of creating children's books.

The emphasis of this book has been on book publishing, with some attention paid to magazines, since they are the traditional stepping stones to book publishing. However, magazine publishing can be fulfilling and rewarding in its own right, especially if you are adept at short story or article writing. Textbook publishers, movie companies, cable TV producers, book packagers, and others also continually need fresh new children's material. Look them up online and in directories in your local library.

An apprentice in any profession takes years to learn his craft. Don't be impatient if you do not begin to publish right away. The day will come when your hard work and careful study pay off. Meanwhile, take pleasure in learning all you can, and you will continue to grow, as a person and as a writer.

CHECKLIST—TAKING AN ACTIVE ROLE

1. Keep writing and working those ideas onto paper.
2. Keep up with publishing news.
3. Join a writers' group.
4. Begin a new work as you wait to hear from a publisher.

SUGGESTIONS—CHAPTER 21

1. Find out which children's writers' conferences will be given in the next year. Find one you can attend either in your geographic area or in a location you plan to visit. What are the requirements for attending? Write to the organizations for further information.

2. Think of ways to start a writers' group that could meet locally on a regular basis. Where would you post notices or run ads to attract fellow writers? Where would you hold your meetings, and how often would you meet?

SOURCES OF SUPPORT
MENTIONED IN THIS CHAPTER
(IN ORDER OF APPEARANCE)

Once Upon a Time . . ., magazine
The Children's Literature Network
The Society of Children's Book Writers and Illustrators

APPENDIX I

Book Lists

There are many good book lists available, including annual listings compiled by organizations devoted to children's literature. A simple search online will direct you to more than you can use. This is just a sampling from tried and true sources.

The Best Children's Books of the Year. A comprehensive 64-page annotated list, published annually, of more than six-hundred titles of fiction and nonfiction for babies and toddlers through age fourteen, arranged by age and category. Bank Street College of Education, 610 West 112th Street, New York, NY 10025.

http://www.bankstreet.edu/bookcom

Caldecott Medal Books and Newbery Medal Books. Annual publication, Association for Library Service to Children (American Library Association), 50 E. Huron Street, Chicago, IL 60611.

http://www.alsc@ala.org

Children's Choices and Young Adults' Choices. Annotated lists of books chosen by children and teenagers annually. International Reading Association, Headquarters Office, 800 Barksdale Road, P.O. Box 8139, Newark, DE 19714-8139.

http://www.reading.org/index.html

Children's Classics. A comprehensive list of both classic and recent books that every parent and child should know from a highly respected publication for those interested in children's literature. The Horn Book, Inc., 56 Roland Street, Suite 200, Boston, MA 02129.

http://www.hbook.com/childclass1.shtml

Notable Children's Books. Annual listing available. Association for Library Service to Children (American Library Association), 50 E. Huron Street, Chicago, IL 60611.

http://www.ala.org

APPENDIX II

Reviews

A good way to learn your way around is to read reviews of current children's books. This list comprises the top reviewers of American children's books today. The publications containing the reviews can be found in most libraries. You can learn about them and their purposes online.

Booklist, American Library Association, 50 E. Huron Street, Chicago, IL 60611
http://www.ala.org/booklist

Bulletin of the Center for Children's Books, 501 East Daniel Street, Champaign, IL 61820
http://alexia.lis.uiuc.edu/puboff/bccb

The Horn Book Magazine, 56 Roland Street, Suite 200, Boston, MA 02129
http://www.hbook.com

Kirkus Reviews, 770 Broadway, New York, NY 10003
http://www.kirkusreviews.com

Publishers Weekly, 245 W. 17th Street, New York, NY 10011
http://www.publishersweekly.com

School Library Journal, 245 W. 17th Street, New York, NY 10011
http://www.schoollibraryjournal.com

VOYA, Voices of Youth Advocates, 4501 Forbes Boulevard, Suite 200, Lanham, MD 20706
http://www.voya.com

APPENDIX III

Children's Literature— History and Criticism

Any of these books will start you off on the rich history of children's books and lead you to others. Should you find any of them out of print, you may be able to find used copies through an online search.

Chukovsky, Kornei. *From Two to Five*. Translated and edited by Miriam Morton. Press, Revised edition, 1963. Written by a leading Russian children's poet in 1925, this work displays the wisdom and insight of a brilliant observer of children.

Hazard, Paul. *Books, Children and Men*, 5th ed. Translated by Marguerite Mitchell. The Horn Book, 1983. A literary celebration of the great stories and tales unique to individual cultures and to childhood.

Lanes, Selma G. *Down the Rabbit Hole*. Atheneum, 1971. Adventures and misadventures in the realm of children's literature.

Marcus, Leonard S. *Dear Genius: The Letters of Ursula Nordstrom*. HarperCollins, 1998.

Meigs, Cornelia. *A Critical History of Children's Literature*. Macmillan, 1953. A survey of children's books in English from earliest times to the present.

Smith, Lillian. *The Unreluctant Years*. American Library Association, 1953. A critical approach to children's literature.

Sutherland, Zena. *Children and Books*, 9th ed. Addison-Wesley, 1997. A children's literature textbook, originally authored by May Hill Arbuthnot.

APPENDIX IV

References

Your personal library should contain a good dictionary and thesaurus, but here are other references you should know about. Look on the Internet as well, using a search engine to find information on various topics, such as copyright, or publishers' catalogs.

Flower, Mary. *A Writer's Guide to a Children's Book Contract.* New York: Fern Hill Books, 1988. Information from a lawyer specializing in children's book contracts, especially helpful for writers who do not have agents.

Herman, Jeff. *Jeff Herman's Guide to Book Publishers, Editors and Literary Agents.* The Writer Books, Kalmbach Publishing Company.

Kozak, Ellen M. *Every Writer's Guide to Copyright and Publishing Law.* Henry Holt, 1990. A primer on U.S. copyright laws (including the burgeoning field of electronic copyright), contracts, libel, fair use, work for hire, collaboration agreements, and dealing with copyright infringement.

Larsen, Michael. *Literary Agents: What They Do, How They Do It, and How to Find and Work with the Right One for You, Revised and Expanded.* New York: John Wiley & Sons, 1996.

Raab, Susan Saltzman. *An Author's Guide to Children's Book Promotion.* Raab Associates, 1999. A guide to getting your book into the hands of those who can influence its sales: teachers, librarians, booksellers, and reviewers.

Ross, Tom, and Marilyn Ross. *The Complete Guide to Self-Publishing: Everything You Need to Know to Write, Publish, Promote and Sell Your Own Book,* 3rd ed. Writers Digest Books, 1994.

Strunk, William, Jr., and E. B. White. *The Elements of Style,* 4th ed. Pearson Allyn & Bacon, 1999. A classic and a must for all writers.

Subject Guide to Children's Books in Print. R. R. Bowker Company. Thorough indexes by subject, title, and author to all books currently in print.
 http://www.bowker.com/bowkerWeb

USA Plays for Kids online at http://usaplays4kids.drury.edu

APPENDIX V

Marketing Information

Children's Book Insider, a monthly newsletter for children's writers, with writing tips and advice, new markets, submission guidance and opportunities, interviews, and practical articles, as well as CWIM updates. Available by subscription.
http://www.write4kids.com

Children's Writer, The Institute of Children's Literature, a monthly newsletter that keeps up-to-date on children's marketing information by maintaining a continuous dialogue with editors and publishers. Available by subscription.
http://www.childrenswriter.com

Children's Writer's & Illustrator's Market (CWIM), Writer's Digest, annual. The best of the market guides, this directory includes contact names, addresses, and submission information for book publishers, magazines, and other markets, plus articles of practical interest to children's writers. Available in bookstores in November for the coming year.
http://www.writersdigest.com/store/books.asp

Meserve, Mollie A., comp. *The Playwright's Companion.* Feedback TheaterBooks, 1991. A submissions guide to theaters and contests in the United States.

Society of Children's Book Writers & Illustrators Bulletin, the bimonthly newsletter of the only children's book organization, with news, articles, and reports about the children's book industry and its creators, including "Publishers' Corner," with new and up-to-date markets. Free to members.
http://www.scbwi.org

APPENDIX VI

Books on the Craft

If you're like me, you'll start reading books on and about writing when you begin your career and continue doing so until the very end. From each book, you may find only one pearl of wisdom, but eventually you'll have a beautiful string of pearls. Don't let out-of-print status on a book discourage you; there are plenty of used bookstores, even some online such as alibris.com, bookfinders.com, and abebooks.com that will help you track it down.

ON WRITING IN GENERAL

Braine, John. *Writing a Novel.* McGraw-Hill, 1975. Braine's methods are encouraging to the writer who does not follow the step-by-step rules laid out by others.

Brande, Dorothea. *Becoming a Writer.* Foreword by John Gardner. J. T. Tarcher, 1981. A compilation of the techniques used by Brande in her creative writing classes in the twenties, yet as timeless as though she were writing today.

Curtis, Richard, and William Thomas Quick. *How to Get Your E-Book Published: An Insider's Guide to the World of Electronic Publishing.* Writers Digest Books, 2002.

Gardner, John. *The Art of Fiction: Notes on Craft for Young Writers.* Knopf, 1984. An outstanding handbook for the aspiring writer about the art and craft of fiction, offering fresh, sensible ideas about where the beginning writer should start.

Goldberg, Natalie. *Writing Down the Bones: Freeing the Writer Within.* Shambhala Publications, 1986. A zen-like guide to writing that is down-to-earth and inspiring.

Highsmith, Patricia. *Plotting and Writing Suspense Fiction.* St. Martin's Press, 1983.

King, Stephen. *On Writing: A Memoir of the Craft.* Pocket Books, 2002. (Also on audiocassette.) A master storyteller shares his thoughts about writing, from his own experience as a successful writer.

Le Guin, Ursula K. *Steering the Craft, Exercises and Discussions on Story Writing for the Lone Navigator or the Mutinous Crew.* Eighth Mountain Press, 1998.

Lukeman, Noah. *The First Five Pages: A Writer's Guide to Staying Out of the Rejection Pile*. Simon & Schuster, 2000.

Sweet, Jeffrey. *The Dramatists' Toolkit*. Heinemann Publishing, 1993.

Sweet, Jeffrey. *Solving Your Script*. Heinemann Publishing, 2001.

On Writing for Children

Alphin, Elaine Marie. *Creating Characters Kids Will Love*. Writer's Digest, 2000. An excellent guide for the beginning writer on creating believable, breathing, characters.

Epstein, Connie C. *The Art of Writing for Children: Skills and Techniques of the Craft*. A former children's book editor emphasizes the importance of good writing.

Giblin, James Cross. *Writing Books for Young People: New Expanded Edition*. The Writer, 1995. A former editor and award-winning nonfiction writer details the stages of developing a book.

Harrison, Barbara, and Gregory Maguire, eds. *Origins of Story: On Writing for Children*. Seventeen notable writers consider how literature, memory, and moral passion serve them in their writings for children.

Karl, Jean E. *How to Write and Sell Children's Picture Books*. Writer's Digest Books, 1994.

Lee, Betsy B. *A Basic Guide to Writing, Selling, and Promoting Children's Books: Plus Information about Self-publishing*.

Lewis, Claudia. *Writing for Young Children*. Doubleday, 1981. Alas, out of print, but search for a used copy.

Livingston, Myra Cohn. *Poem-Making: Ways to Begin Writing Poetry*. HarperCollins, 1991.

Naylor, Phyllis Reynolds. *The Craft of Writing a Novel*. The Writer, Inc., 1989. An award-winning author draws on her own experience to show the way to produce a solid story with believable characters.

Nixon, Joan Lowery. *Writing Mysteries for Young People*. The Writer, 1977. If you're thinking of writing mysteries, this is a must, written by a master.

Shepard, Aaron. *The Business of Writing for Children: An Award-Winning Author's Tips on Writing and Publishing Children's Books, or How to Write, Publish, and Promote a Book for Kids*. An experienced and award-winning author provides a wealth of tips on how to write, sell, and promote books.

Suen, Anastasia. *Picture Writing: A New Approach to Writing for Kids and Teens*. Writer's Digest, 2003. An experienced writer approaches the craft of writing through creating vivid images with words.

Underdown, Harold D. *The Complete Idiot's Guide to Publishing Children's Books.* Indianapolis: Alpha, 2004.

Wyndham, Lee. *Writing for Children & Teenagers.* 3rd ed. revised by Arnold Madison. Writer's Digest, 1989. An excellent basic guide to writing for children, including how to organize a book.

Yolen, Jane. *Take Joy: A Book for Writers.* The Writer, 2003. Replaces Yolen's *Writing Books for Children.* A veteran writer for children celebrates her chosen profession by sharing insights and sage advice.

For Those Who Also Illustrate

Amoss, Berthe, and Eric Suben. *Writing & Illustrating Children's Books for Publication: Two Perspectives.* A lively and helpful book in which a writer and an illustrator share their insights in creating a children's book.

Gates, Frieda. *How to Write, Illustrate and Design Children's Books.* Lloyd-Simone, 1986.

Shulevitz, Uri. *Writing with Pictures: How to Write and Illustrate Children's Books.* Watson-Guptill, 1985.

You may find any number of valuable sites online for the illustrator. Here are a couple to get you started. Look up artists whose work you admire by typing their names in a search engine; many have Web sites of their own, and offer insights into various illustration techniques.

Illustrating Children's Books. The Children's Book Council Web site: http://www.cbcbooks.org/html/illustrating.html

SaneDraw's "Illustrating Children's Picture Books," on a Web site maintained by Sandro Corsi based on his course for illustrators: http://www.sanedraw.com/ILPICBKS/002CLSRS.HTM

Writing, Illustrating, and Publishing Children's Books. The Purple Crayon: http://www.underdown.org

Some regional groups of the Society of Children's Book Writers sponsor special "Illustrator Days" at which artists can show their portfolios and hear professional illustrators, editors, and art directors talk about the illustrator's place in children's books. Check it out at the organization's Web site: http://www.scbwi.org

APPENDIX VII

Services, Studies, and Support

ORGANIZATIONS

The Author's Guild, a society of published authors advocating free speech, fair compensation, and copyright protection. http://www.authorsguild.org

The Children's Book Council, a nonprofit trade organization dedicated to encouraging literacy and the use and enjoyment of children's books. Their Members List includes publishers' addresses, phone numbers, and editors' names. http://www.cbcbooks.org

The National Writers Union, the only labor union that represents freelance writers in all genres, formats, and media. The National Writers Union, 113 University Place, 6th Floor, New York, NY 10003. http://www.nwu.org

PEN, a major voice of the literary community that seeks to defend the freedom of expression wherever it may be threatened. http://www.pen.org

Poets & Writers, Inc., a nonprofit organization for poets, performance poets, fiction writers, and writers of literary nonfiction. http://www.pw.org

The Society of Children's Book Writers and Illustrators, the only organization devoted solely to serving children's writers and illustrators. Society of Children's Book Writers and Illustrators, 8271 Beverly Boulevard, Los Angeles, CA 90048. http://www.scbwi.org

DEGREE STUDIES

Some colleges now offer advanced degrees in writing for children. These are some you may want to explore:

Vermont College offers a brief residency MFA program in Writing for Children and Young Adults. Vermont College, 36 College Street, Montpelier, VT 05602

Spalding University in Louisville, Kentucky, also offers a brief residency Master of Fine Arts in Writing program. Spalding University, 851 S. Fourth St., Louisville, KY 40203

The New School in New York City offers a full time MFA program in Creative Writing with a concentration in Writing for Children. The New School Graduate Writing Program, 66 West 12th Street, New York, NY 10011

Support

The Manuscript Workshop with Barbara Seuling. A writing workshop in Vermont for people who are serious about writing for children. To find out more about The Manuscript Workshop, check out the Web site at www.themanuscriptworkshop.com

Once Upon a Time ... Magazine. Audrey Baird, editor. A quarterly support magazine edited by children's author Audrey Baird, in which writers talk to and support each other in their struggle to be published writers. Excellent support from fellow writers and several columnists—professional authors, illustrators, editors, art directors, and so forth—who provide advice, information, and encouragement from their various vantage points. 553 Winston Court, St. Paul, MN 55118. E-mail: audreyouat@comcast.net. http://once-uponatimemag.com

Good Web Sites for Children's Writers

The nature of the Internet is rapid change, so some of these addresses may be gone by the time you look them up, but they are among the more stable that I've found. Once you hook up to one, you will probably find links to others that are just as helpful.

http://www.acs.ucalgary.ca/~dkbrown
    A site maintained by David K. Brown of the University of Calgary
http://www.bartleby.com
    An Internet publisher of literature, reference, and verse, providing access to books and information free of charge.
http://www.childrensliteraturenetwork.org
    Children's Literature Network, created as a nonprofit membership organization for writers and others interested in children's literature; a generous portion of their site is open to nonmembers.
http://www.education.wisc.edu/ccbc
    The Cooperative Children's Book Center at the University of Wisconsin; you can join their monthly book discussions by registering at no cost.

http://www.institutechildrenslit.com
> Weekly chats and helpful articles for children's writers, run by the Institute of Children's Literature.

http://www.underdown.org
> The informative site of Harold Underdown, editor, called The Purple Crayon.

http://www.writerswrite.com/publishing
> Writers Write sponsored by iUniverse.

APPENDIX VIII

Even More Titles by Genre

Many book titles have been mentioned throughout this book to encourage you to read them yourself. Picking up a book and reading it will help to retain what you've learned for a long time.

Here are some additional titles from recent readings and reviews that represent excellence in every category and age. It is inevitable that some cross categories, but they are listed under what I felt was the more dominant aspect of the book. Continue to read and follow authors and illustrators as they interest you. This foundation will be a valuable asset in your writing future.

BABY BOOKS

Reading, for a baby, is the experience of hearing the loving sounds, in undulating rhythms, of a parent's voice, while nestling cozily in his or her arms. These happy associations expand as images are introduced, in bold colors and shapes. That is why most of the books listed feature simple crooning texts or soft lyrical phrases, as well as baby games with fingers, toes, chins, and belly buttons.

Appelt, Kathi. *Oh My Baby, My Little One,* illustrated by Jane Dyer. Harcourt, 2000.

Bauer, Marion Dane. *Love Song for a Baby,* illustrated by Dan Andreasen. Simon & Schuster, 2002.

Bradman, Tony. *Daddy's Lullaby,* illustrated by Jason Cockcroft. Margaret K. McElderry, 2002.

Brown, Margaret Wise. *Goodnight Moon,* illustrated by Clement Thacher Hurd. Harper & Row, 1947.

Chorao, Kay. *The Baby's Lap Book.* Dutton, 1991.

Dunrae, Oliver. *Gossie & Gertie.* Houghton Mifflin, 2002.

Fox, Mem. *Time for Bed,* illustrated by Jane Dyer. Gulliver Books, 1993.

Glazer, Tom. *Eye Winker, Tom Tinker, Chin Chopper: 50 Musical Fingerplays.* Doubleday, 1992.

Hoban, Tana. *Black on White.* Greenwillow, 1993.

Intrater, Roberta Grobel. *Peek-a-Boo.* Cartwheel Books, 1997.

Katz, Karen. *Where Is Baby's Belly Button?* Little Simon, 2000.

Lewis, Rose A. *I Love You Like Crazy Cakes*, illustrated by Jane Dyer. Little Brown, 2000.

Meyers, Susan. *Everywhere Babies*. Harcourt, 2001.

Miller, Margaret. *Big and Little*. Greenwillow, 1998.

Perkins, Al. *Hand, Hand, Fingers, Thumb*, illustrated by Eric Gurney. Random House, 1998.

Spinelli, Eileen. *When Mama Comes Home Tonight*, illustrated by Jane Dyer. Simon & Schuster, 1998.

Suen, Anastasia. *Baby Born*, illustrated by Chih-Wei Chang. Lee & Low, 1999.

Taylor, Ann. *Baby Dance*, illustrated by Marjorie van Heerden. Harper-Festival, 1999.

Thompson, Lauren. *Little Quack*, illustrated by Derek Anderson. Simon & Schuster, 2003.

Williams, Vera B. *More More More Said the Baby*, Greenwillow, 1990.

BOARD BOOKS

Many picture books are now reissued as board books. While some do beautifully in the board format, some are shortened versions to fit the format. Check these out against the originals before purchasing if you want to be sure to get the original text and illustrations.

Ahlberg, Janet, and Allan Ahlberg. *Peek-a-Boo!* Viking, 1997.

Apperley, Dawn. *Hello Little Lamb*. David & Charles Children's Books, 2000.

Archambault, John, and Bill Martin, Jr. *Chicka Chicka ABC*, illustrated by Lois Ehlert, Little Simon, 1993.

Bang, Molly. *Ten, Nine, Eight*. Greenwillow, 1998.

Barton, Byron. *The Three Bears Board Book*. HarperFestival, 1997.

Boynton, Sandra. *Moo, Baa, La La La*. Little Simon, 1982.

Brown, Margaret Wise. *Goodnight Moon*, illustrated by Clement Thacher Hurd. HarperCollins, 1991.

Carle, Eric. *The Very Hungry Caterpillar*. Philomel, 1969/Putnam, 1994.

Cimarusti, Marie Torres. *Peek-a-Moo*. Dutton, 1998.

Cohen, Miriam. *Say Hi, Backpack Baby!* Starbright Books, 2002.

Cummings, Pat. *My Aunt Came Back*. HarperFestival, 1998.

Ehlert, Lois. *Color Zoo Board Book*. HarperFestival, 1997.

Hines-Stephens, Sarah. *Bean Soup*, illustrated by Anna Grossnickle Hines. Red Wagon Books, 2000.

Hubbell, Patricia. *Pots and Pans*, illustrated by Diane deGroat. Harper-Festival, 1998.

Hutchins, Pat. *Rosie's Walk*. Random House, 1998.

Keats, Ezra Jack. *The Snowy Day*. Viking, 1996.

Lindgren, Barbro. *Sam's Teddy Bear*, illustrated by Eva Eriksson. Morrow, 1982.

Miranda, Anne. *To Market, To Market*, illustrated by Janet Stevens. Harcourt, 1997.

Oxenbury, Helen. *Shopping Trip*. Dial, 1991.

Root, Phyllis. *One Duck Stuck*, illustrated by Jane Chapman. Candlewick, 2001.

Tougas, Chris. *The Hungry Pig: Wacky Farm (Fun Works)*, illustrated by Ron C. Lipking. Mouse Works, 1997.

Tracy, Tom. *Show Me*, illustrated by Darcia Labrosse. HarperFestival, 1999.

Trapani, Iza. *Shoo Fly*. Charlesbridge, 2002.

Uff, Caroline. *Lulu's Busy Day*. Walker & Co, 2000.

Wells, Rosemary. *Max's Bedtime*. Dutton, 1998.

Yolen, Jane. *How Do Dinosaurs Say Good Night?* illustrations by Mark Teague. Blue Sky, 2000.

TODDLER BOOKS

These are books for those beyond baby books, yet not quite up to the sophisticated level of traditional picture books. Toddler books, sometimes found in chunky board book versions, are a child's first real experience with books as books, not as chewable toys.

Aigner-Clark, Julie. *Baby Einstein: Pretty Poems and Wonderful Words*, illustrated by Nadeem Zaidi. Hyperion, 2003.

Archambault, John. *Chicka Chicka Boom Boom*, illustrated by Bill Martin Jr., Simon & Schuster, 1991.

Brown, Margaret Wise. *The Runaway Bunny*, illustrated by Clement Hurd. HarperCollins, 1974.

Buzzeo, Toni. *Dawdle Duckling*, illustrated by Margaret Spengler. Dial, 2003.

Capucilli, Alyssa Satin. *The Potty Book*, illustrated by Dorothy Stott. Barrons Juveniles, 2000.

Christelow, Eileen. *Five Little Monkeys Jumping on the Bed*. Houghton Mifflin, 1998.

Cole, Joanna. *I'm a Big Brother*, illustrated by Maxie Chambliss. Morrow, 1997.

Cowley, Joy. *Mrs. Wishy Washy's Farm*, illustrated by Elizabeth Fuller. Philomel, 2003.

Crews, Nina. *One Hot Summer Day*. Greenwillow, 1995.

Davis, Katie. *Who Hops?* Harcourt, 1998.

Degen, Bruce. *Jamberry*. HarperFestival, 1995.

Hest, Amy. *Kiss Good Night*, illustrated by Anita Jeram. Walker, 2001.

Hill, Eric. *Hello Spot*. Putnam, 2004.

Martin, Bill Jr. *Brown Bear, Brown Bear, What Do You See?* illustrated by Eric Carle. Henry Holt & Company, 1992.

Murphy, Mary. *I Kissed the Baby!* Candlewick, 2003.

Rockwell, Lizzy. *Hello Baby!* Dragonfly, 2000.

Rosen, Michael. *We're Going on a Bear Hunt,* illustrated by Helen Oxenbury. Little Simon/Aladdin, 1992.

Santoro, Christopher. *Open the Barn Door, Find a Cow.* Random House, 1993.

Scarry, Richard. *Richard Scarry's Best Mother Goose Ever.* Golden Books, 1998.

Schwartz, Amy. *What James Likes Best.* Atheneum, 2003.

Seuling, Barbara. *Winter Lullaby.* Harcourt, 1998.

Szykeres, Cyndy. *I Can Count 100 Bunnies: and So Can You.* Cartwheel, 1999.

PICTURE BOOKS—FICTION

Read the old along with the new, for a sense of what makes a picture book last through the decades. You will find the beloved classics, like *Where the Wild Things Are,* on every book list, so I am including recent books that will give you a sense of what's happening now. Continue to search out the best books each year and keep up-to-date with what's being published.

Appelt, Kathie. *Bubba and Beau, Best Friends,* illustrated by Arthur Howard. Harcourt, 2002.

Bryan, Ashley. *Beautiful Blackbird.* Atheneum, 2003.

Christelow, Eileen. *The Great Pig Search.* Clarion, 2001.

Cronin, Doreen. *Diary of a Worm,* illustrated by Harry Bliss. HarperCollins, 2003.

Falconer, Ian. *Olivia,* Atheneum, 2000.

Hershenhorn, Esther. *Fancy That,* illustrated by Megan Lloyd. Holiday House, 2003.

Kao, K. T. *One Pizza, One Penny,* translated by Roxanne Feldman, illustrated by Giuliano Ferri. Cricket Books, 2003.

Lewin, Betsy. *Click, Clack, Moo: Cows that Type.* Simon & Schuster, 2000.

Manushkin, Fran. *Baby, Come Out!* illustrated by Ron Himler. Starbright, 2002.

Mazer, Anne. *The Salamander Room,* illustrated by Steve Johnson. Knopf, 1991.

Moss, Lloyd. *Zin! Zin! Zin! A Violin,* illustrated by Marjorie Priceman. Simon & Schuster, 1995.

Partridge, Elizabeth. *Kogi's Mysterious Journey,* illustrated by Aki Sogabe. Dutton, 2003.

Rohmann, Eric. *My Friend Rabbit.* Roaring Brook, 2002.

Root, Phyllis. *Big Mama Makes the World,* illustrated by Helen Oxenbury. Walker, 2002.

Seuling, Barbara. *Whose House?* Harcourt, 2004.

Shannon, David. *No, David!* Scholastic, 1998.

Sis, Peter. *Fire Truck.* Greenwillow, 1998.

Steig, William. *Pete's a Pizza.* HarperCollins, 1998.

Watson, Clyde. *Father Fox's Pennyrhymes,* illustrated by Wendy Watson. HarperCollins, 2001.

Wells, Rosemary. *Noisy Nora.* Dial, 1999.

Willems, Mo. *Don't Let the Pigeon Drive the Bus!* Hyperion, 2003.

Williams, Vera. *A Chair for My Mother.* Greenwillow, 1982.

Woodson, Jacqueline. *Visiting Day.* Scholastic, 2002.

PICTURE BOOKS—NONFICTION

Picture books that are factual are not just for the very young reader. You will find in this list some that will appeal to the four-year-old and some that will be more suited to the ten-year-old. Beautifully illustrated books serve as a child's first introduction to complex subjects, and provide solid information equally through text and pictures; subject matter generally dictates the interest level of the reader.

Anderson, M. T. *Strange Mr. Satie,* illustrated by Petra Mathers. Viking, 2003.

Chanda, Deborah, and Madeleine Comora. *George Washington's Teeth,* illustrated by Brock Cole. Farrar, Straus & Giroux, 2003.

Gerstein, Mordecai. *The Man Who Walked between the Towers,* Roaring Brook, 2004.

Gomi, Taro. *Everyone Poops,* Kane/Miller, 1993.

Greenberg, Jan, and Sandra Jordan. *Action Jackson,* illustrated by Robert Andrew Parker. Millbrook Press, 2002.

Kalman, Maira. *Fireboat: The Heroic Adventures of the John J. Harvey.* Putnam's, 2002.

Krull, Kathy. *Harvesting Hope: The Story of Cesar Chavez,* illustrated by Yuyi Morales. Harcourt, 2003.

Martin, Jacqueline Briggs. *Snowflake Bentley,* illustrated by Mary Azarian. Houghton Mifflin, 1998.

Myers, Walter Dean. *Blues Journey,* illustrated by Christopher Myers. Holiday House, 2003.

Orgill, Roxane. *If I Only Had a Horn: Young Louis Armstrong,* illustrated by Leonard Jenkins. Houghton Mifflin, 2002.

Ryan, Pamela Munoz. *When Marian Sang: The True Recital of Marian Andersen,* illustrated by Brian Selznick. Scholastic, 2002.

Seuling, Barbara. *Winter Lullaby.* Harcourt, 1998.

Singer, Marilyn. *Prairie Dogs Kiss and Lobsters Wave: How Animals Say Hello,* illustrated by Normand Chartier. Holt, 1998.

Stanley, Diane. *Leonardo Da Vinci.* William Morrow, 1996.

Suen, Anastasia. *Man on the Moon,* illustrated by Benrei Huang. Viking, 1997.

Swinburne, Stephen R. *Lots and Lots of Zebra Stripes.* Boyds Mills Press, 2002.

Warhola, James. *Uncle Andy's.* Putnam's, 2003.

Willard, Nancy. *Pish, Posh, Said Hieronymus Bosch,* illustrated by Diane and Leo Dillon. Harcourt, 1991.

EASY-TO-READ BOOKS

Good stories and information in short easy-to-read books have been a challenge to writers since these books were first introduced. Now a solid part of every child's library, old favorites as well as recent publications continue to provide exciting reading for beginning readers.

Alphin, Elaine Marie. *Dinosaur Hunter,* illustrated by Don Bolognese. HarperCollins, 2003.

Bonsall, Crosby. *The Case of the Hungry Stranger,* HarperCollins, 2002.

Brenner, Martha. *Abe Lincoln's Hat,* illustrated by Donald Cook. Random House, 1994.

Donnelly, Judy. *Moonwalk: The First Trip to the Moon,* illustrated with photographs by Dennis Davidson. Random House, 1989.

Eastman, P. D. *Are You My Mother?* Random House, 1960.

Geisert, Arthur. *Oink.* Houghton, 1991.

Hautzig, Deborah. *Little Witch Learns to Read,* illustrated by Sylvia Wickstrom. Random House, 2003.

Laurence, Daniel. *Captain and Matey Set Sail.* HarperCollins, 2003.

Little, Jean. *Emma's Strange Pet,* illustrated by Jennifer Plecas. Harper-Collins, 2003.

Lobel, Arnold. *Frog and Toad Are Friends,* HarperCollins, 1970.

Milton, Joyce. *Gorillas,* illustrated by Bryn Barnard. Random House, 1997.

Murphy, Frank. *George Washington and the General's Dog,* illustrated by Richard Walz. Random House, 2002.

Parrish, Peggy. *Amelia Bedelia,* Harper & Row, 1967.

Rosenbloom, Joseph. *Deputy Dan and the Bank Robbers.* Random House, 1985.

Ruiz, Aristides. *Green Eggs and Ham,* illustrated by Dr. Seuss. Random House, 1960.

Rylant, Cynthia. *Henry and Mudge* (series). Simon, 1998.

Slater, Teddy. *The Littles Go on a Hike,* illustrated by Jacqueline Rogers. Scholastic, 2002.

Spirn, Michele. *The Know-Nothings,* illustrated by R. W. Alley. Harper Trophy, 1997.

Standiford, Natalie. *The Bravest Dog Ever: the True Story of Balto,* illustrated by Donald Cook. Random House, 1989.

Suen, Anastasia. *Loose Tooth,* illustrated by Allan Eitzen, created by Ezra Jack Keats. Puffin, 2003.

Thomas, Shelley Moore. *Good Night, Good Knight,* illustrated by Jennifer Plecas. Dutton, 2000.

EARLY CHAPTER BOOKS

These are for children just becoming hungry independent readers at the young end of the elementary school years. These books are lighter than standard middle-grade books in terms of appearance (larger type size and shorter chapters) as well as content, where even serious subjects are given a gentle touch, and humor plays an important role.

Adler, David A. *Cam Jansen* (series). Viking, 1998.

Brinley, Bertrand R. *The Mad Scientists' Club,* illustrated by Charles Geer. Purple House Press, 2001.

Cameron, Ann. *Gloria Rising,* illustrated by Lis Toft. Frances Foster, 2002.

Christopher, Matt. *Soccer Cats* (series). Little, Brown.

Duey, Kathleen. *The Journey Home,* illustrated by Omar Rayyan. Aladdin, 2003.

Fine, Anne. *The Jamie and Angus Stories,* illustrated by Penny Dale. Candlewick, 2002.

Giff, Patricia Reilly. *The Kids of the Polk Street School* (series). Yearling.

Jukes, Mavis. *No One Is Going to Nashville,* illustrated by Lloyd Bloom. Knopf, 1983.

Kline, Suzy. *Herbie Jones,* illustrated by Richard Williams. Putnam, 1985.

Lottridge, Celia Barker. *Berta: A Remarkable Dog,* illustrated by Elsa Myotte. Groundwood, 2002.

Lovelace, Maud Hart. *Betsy-Tacy,* illustrated by Lois Lenski. Harper & Row, 1940.

McDonald, Megan. *Judy Moody* (& sequels), illustrated by Peter Reynolds. Candlewick, 2002.

Morgenstern, Susie. *Princesses Are People, Too,* illustrated by Serge Bloch. Viking, 2002.

Osbourne, Mary Pope. *The Magic Tree House* (series). Random House.

Park, Barbara. *Junie B. Jones: One-Man Band,* illustrated by Denise Brunkis. Random House, 2003.

Pilkey, David. *Captain Underpants* (series). Blue Sky.

Sachar, Louis. *Sideways Stories from Wayside School.* HarperTrophy, 1998.

Seuling, Barbara. *Oh No, It's Robert* (& sequels), illustrated by Paul Brewer. Cricket Books, 1999.

Sharmat, Marjorie Weinman. *Nate the Great* (series). Delacorte.

Stample, Judith Bauer. *Dinosaur Detectives,* illustrated by Ted Enik. Scholastic, 2002.

Willner-Pardo, Gina. *Spider Storch's Fumbled Field Trip.* Whitman, 1998.

MIDDLE-GRADE FICTION

When you're choosing fiction to read, by all means read those books that have won awards and are on recommended reading lists, but don't forget current titles by your favorite authors, or books that have been singled out by reviewers for their unique voice, fine writing, or remarkable insights. Choose a few that look like just plain fun. You'll find a little of everything here from recent titles, but add your own.

Auch, Mary Jane. *I Was a Third Grade Spy,* illustrated by Herm Auch. Holiday House, 2001.

Avi, Crispin. *The Cross of Lead.* Hyperion, 2002.

Creech, Sharon. *Ruby Holler.* HarperCollins, 2002.

DiCamillo, Kate. *Because of Winn-Dixie.* Candlewick, 2001.

Funke, Cornelia. *Inkheart.* Translated by Anthea Bell. Scholastic, 2003.

Giff, Patricia Reilly. *Pictures of Hollis Woods.* Random House, 2002.

Hansen, Joyce. *I Thought My Soul Would Rise & Fly: the Diary of Patsy, a Freed Girl* (Dear America Series). Scholastic, 1997.

Henkes, Kevin. *Olive's Ocean.* Greenwillow, 2003.

Holt, Kimberley Willis. *Dancing in Cadillac Light.* Putnam, 2001.

Horvath, Polly. *Everything on a Waffle.* Farrar, Straus & Giroux, 2001.

Ibbotson, Eva. *Journey to the River Sea,* illustrated by Kevin Hawkes. Dutton, 2002.

Ketchum, Liza. *Orphan Journey Home.* HarperCollins, 2000.

Lowry, Lois. *The Silent Boy,* Houghton Mifflin, 2003.

Marsden, Carolyn. *The Gold Threaded Dress.* Candlewick, 2002.

Mazer, Harry. *A Boy at War: A Novel of Pearl Harbor.* Simon & Schuster, 2001.

McKay, Hilary. *Saffy's Angel.* Simon & Schuster, 2002.

Nelson, Teresa. *Ruby Electric.* Atheneum, 2003.

Park, Linda Sue. *When My Name Was Keoko: A Novel of Korea in World War II.* Clarion, 2002.

Paterson, Katherine. *The Same Stuff as Stars.* Clarion, 2002.

Pullman, Phillip. *The Amber Spyglass* (trilogy). Knopf, 2000.

Rowling, J. K. *Harry Potter* (series). Scholastic.

Ryan, Pamela Munoz. *Esperanza Rising.* Scholastic, 2000.

Tolan, Stephanie S. *Surviving the Applewhites.* HarperCollins, 2002.

Williams, Vera. *Amber Was Brave, Essie Was Smart.* Greenwillow, 2001.
Winkler, Henry, and Lin Oliver. *Hank Zipzer* (series), Putnam.

MIDDLE-GRADE NONFICTION

Readers in the middle grades are the most voracious readers of all, and will devour books on any subject that strikes their interest, even if their experience falls short of understanding some of the more complex issues. A glance at this list will give you some idea of the range of interest of middle-grade readers.

Alvarez, Mark. *The Official Baseball Hall of Fame Story of Jackie Robinson.* Simon & Schuster, 1990.
Anderson, M. T. *Handel: He Knew What He Liked.* Candlewick, 2001.
Dash, Joan. *The Longitude Prize: The Race between Moon and Watch-Machine,* illustrated by Dusan Petricic. Frances Foster, 2000.
Fleming, Candace. *Ben Franklin's Almanac: Being a True Account of the Good Gentleman's Life.* Atheneum, 2003.
Google, e.encyclopedia, DK Publishing, 2003.
Haas, Jessie. *Fire! My Parents' Story.* Greenwillow, 1998.
Hansen, Joyce. *Women of Hope: African Americans Who Made a Difference.* Scholastic, 1998.
Krull, Kathleen. *The Boy on Fairfield Street: How Ted Geisel Grew Up to Be Dr. Seuss,* illustrated by Steve Johnson and Lou Fancher. Random House, 2004.
————. *Lives of . . .* (series on presidents, musicians, athletes, etc.) Harcourt.
Lasky, Kathryn. *The Man Who Made Time Travel,* illustrated by Kevin Hawkes. Farrar, Straus & Giroux, 2003.
Lawton, Clive A. *Auschwitz: The Story of a Nazi Death Camp,* Candlewick, 2002.
Levine, Ellen. *Freedom's Children: Young Civil Rights Activists Tell Their Own Stories.* Putnam, 1993.
Murphy, Jim. *Inside the Alamo.* Delacorte, 2003.
Schwartz, David M. *Millions to Measure,* illustrated by Steven Kellogg. HarperCollins, 2003.
Seuling, Barbara. *From Head to Toe: The Amazing Human Body and How It Works,* illustrated by Ed Miller. Holiday House, 2002.
Sis, Peter. *The Tree of Life: A Book Depicting the Life of Charles Darwin, Naturalist, Geologist & Thinker.* Farrar, Straus & Giroux, 2003.
Swinburne, Stephen R. *Once a Wolf: How Biologists Fought to Bring Back the Gray Wolf,* photographed by Jim Brandenburg. Houghton Mifflin, 1999.
Terban, Marvin. *The Scholastic Dictionary of Idioms,* illustrated by John Devore. Scholastic, 1996.

Teenage or Young Adult Fiction

Today's young adult books deal with everything from strong personal issues to wacky humor. Acceptance is a big theme, as young people—sometimes on the edge—search for their place in the universe. I've included a couple of older titles by Robert Cormier and Nancy Garden so you can include these landmark books in your reading.

Anderson, Laurie Halse. *Speak*. Farrar, Straus & Giroux, 1999.

Anderson, M. T. *Feed*. Candlewick, 2002.

Block, Francesca Lia. *Wasteland*. HarperCollins, 2003.

Brashares, Ann. *The Sisterhood of the Traveling Pants*. Random House, 2001.

Brooks, Martha. *True Confessions of a Heartless Girl*. Farrar, Straus & Giroux, 2003.

Chambers, Aiden. *Dance on My Grave*. Random House, 1995.

Coman, Carolyn. *Many Stones*. Front Street, 2000.

Cormier, Robert. *The Chocolate War*. Knopf, 1974.

Crutcher, Chris. *Whale Talk*. Greenwillow, 2001.

DuPrau, Jeanne. *City of Ember*. Random House, 2003.

Flinn, Alex. *Breathing Underwater*. HarperCollins, 2001.

Garden, Nancy. *Annie on my Mind*. Farrar, Straus & Giroux, 1982.

Hoffman, Alice. *Green Angel*. Scholastic, 2003.

Holt, Kimberly Willis. *Keeper of the Night*. Holt, 2003.

Jenkins A. M. *Out of Order*. HarperCollins, 2003.

Lerangis, Peter. *Smiler's Bones*. Scholastic, 2005.

Levithan, David. *Boy Meets Boy*. Knopf, 2003.

Martin, Ann M. *A Corner of the Universe*. Scholastic, 2002.

Mazer, Norma Fox. *Girlhearts*. HarperCollins, 2001.

McDonald, Janet. *Twists and Turns*. Farrar, Straus & Giroux, 2003.

Myers, Walter Dean. *Shooter*. Amistad Press, 2004.

Myracle, Lauren. *Kissing Kate*. Penguin Putnam, 2003.

Na, An. *One Step to Heaven*. Front Street, 2001.

Peck, Richard. *The River between Us*. Penguin Putnam, 2003.

Peters, Julie Anne. *Keeping You a Secret: A Novel*. Megan Tingley, 2003.

Sanchez, Alex. *Rainbow Boys*. Simon & Schuster, 2001.

Wolf, Virginia Euwer. *True Believer*. Atheneum, 2001.

Teenage or Young Adult Nonfiction

Teenagers and young adults read books published for adults as well as these titles categorized as young adult. That gives you some idea of what to expect from these books. The difference is often merely a matter of whether the subject matter comes up in the curriculum or the life or the curiosity of the reader.

Albert, Martin. *Sitting Bull and His World*. Dutton, 2000.

Anderson, Stephen. *So You Wanna Be a Rock Star?: How to Create Music, Get Gigs, and Maybe Even Make It Big!* illustrated by Zachary Snyder. Beyond Words, 1999.

Appelt, Kathi. *Poems from Homeroom: A Writer's Place to Start*. Holt, 2002.

Aronson, Marc. *Sir Walter Raleigh and the Quest for El Dorado*. Clarion, 2000.

Chambers, Aidan. *Postcards from No Man's Land*. Dutton, 2002.

Crutcher, Chris. *King of the Mild Frontier: An Ill-Advised Autobiography*. HarperCollins, 2003.

Eire, Carlos. *Waiting for Snow in Havana: Confessions of a Cuban Boy*. Free Press, 2004.

Freedman, Russell. *In Defense of Liberty: The Story of America's Bill of Rights*. Holiday House, 2003.

Giblin, James Cross. *The Life and Death of Adolf Hitler*. Clarion, 2003.

Greenberg, Jan and Sandra Jordan. *Runaway Girl: The Artist Louise Bourgeois*. Harry Abrams, 2003.

Ketchum, Liza. *Into the New Country: Eight Remarkable Women of the West*. Little Brown, 2000.

Levine, Ellen. *Darkness over Denmark: The Danish Resistance and the Rescue of the Jews*. Holiday House, 2000.

Myers, Walter Dean. *Bad Boy: A Memoir*. HarperCollins, 2001.

Orgill, Roxane. *Shout, Sister, Shout: Ten Girl Singers Who Shaped a Century*. Margaret K. McElderry, 2001.

Partridge, Elizabeth. *This Land Was Made for You and Me: The Life & Songs of Woody Guthrie*. Penguin Putnam, 2003.

Paulsen, Gary. *How Angel Peterson Got His Name and Other Outrageous Tales about Extreme Sports*. Random House, 2003.

Philbrick, Nathaniel. *Revenge of the Whale: The True Story of the Whaleship* Essex. Putnam, 2002.

Reef, Catherine. *Sigmund Freud: Pioneer of the Mind*. Clarion, 2001.

Winick, Judd. *Pedro and Me: Friendship, Loss, and What I Learned*. Holt, 2000.

SHORT STORIES

A book of short stories can be a collection of a single author's work or several stories solicited by one person who acts as the editor, on a particular theme. It can also be a collection of already published stories on a theme.

Middle Grade

Armstrong, Jennifer. *What a Song Can Do: 12 Riffs on the Power of Music*. Knopf, 2004.

Asher, Sandy. *On Her Way: Stories and Poems about Growing up Girl.* Dutton, 2004.

Dahl, Roald. *The Wonderful Story of Henry Sugar and Six More,* illustrated by Quentin Blake. Knopf, 2001.

Hurston, Zora Neale. *The Skull Talks Back and Other Haunting Tales,* illustrated by Leonard Jenkins. HarperCollins, 2004.

Hurwitz, Johanna. *Birthday Surprises: Ten Great Stories to Unwrap.* Morrow, 1995.

Jones, Diana Wynne. *Stopping for a Spell,* illustrated by Mark Zug. Greenwillow, 2004.

Mazer, Harry. *The Dog in the Freezer: Three Novellas.* Aladdin, 1998.

Mercado, Nancy, ed. *Tripping over the Lunch Lady and Other School Stories.* Dial, 2004.

Peck, Richard. *What If? A Collection of Stories.* Dial, 2004.

St. Antoine, Sara, ed. *Stories from Where We Live—The Great Lakes,* illustrated by Trudy Nicholson (and similar anthologies for different regions of the United States). Milkweed, 2003.

San Souci, Robert D. *A Terrifying Taste of Short & Shivery: Thirty Creepy Tales,* illustrated by Katherine Coville. Delacorte, 1998.

Young Adult

Appelt, Kathi. *Kissing Tennessee: and Other Stories from the Stardust Dance.* Harcourt, 2000.

Bauer, Marion Dane, ed. *Am I Blue?: Coming Out from the Silence,* illustrated by Beck Underwood. HarperCollins, 1999.

Byars, Betsy, comp. *Top Teen Stories,* illustrated by Robert Geary. Kingfisher, 2004.

Gallo, Donald R., ed. *Destination Unexpected: Short Stories.* Candlewick, 2003.

Myers, Walter Dean. *A Time to Love: Stories from the Old Testament.* Scholastic, 2003.

POETRY

The books listed here are not just collections, either on a theme by one author, or in anthologies. There are biographies told in poems, whole books devoted to one poem, and novels written in free verse. Many picture books are written in verse; some are listed among regular picture books.

Aguado, Bill. *Paint Me Like I Am: Teen Poems from WritersCorps.* HarperTempest, 2003.

Baird, Audrey B. *Storm Coming,* illustrated by Patrick O'Brien. Boyds Mills Press, 2001.

de Regniers, Beatrice Schenk & others. *Sing a Song of Popcorn: Every Child's Book of Poems,* illustrated by nine Caldecott Medalists. Scholastic, 1988.

Fleischman, Paul. *Joyful Noise,* illustrated by Eric Beddows. Harper-Collins, 1992.

Haas, Jessie. *Horseprints: Horse Poems.* Greenwillow, 2004.

Hopkins, Lee Bennett, ed. *Hoofbeats, Claws, and Rippled Fins: Creature Poems,* illustrated by Stephen Alcorn. HarperCollins, 2002.

Kennedy, X. J. *Exploding Gravy: Poems to Make You Laugh,* illustrated by Joy Allen. Little, Brown, 2002.

Kuskin, Karla. *Moon, Have You Met My Mother?* illustrated by Sergio Ruzzier. HarperCollins, 2003.

Moore, Lilian. *Sunflakes: Poems for Children,* illustrated by Jan Ormerod. Clarion, 1992.

Nelson, Marilyn. *Carver: A Life in Poems.* Front Street, 2001.

Nye, Naomi Shihab. *19 Varieties of Gazelle: Poems of the Middle East.* Greenwillow, 2002.

Prelutsky, Jack. *If Not for the Cat,* illustrated by Ted Rand. Greenwillow, 2004.

Rylant, Cynthia. *God Went to Beauty School.* HarperTempest, 2003.

Sidman, Joyce. *The World According to Dog: Poems and Teen Voices.* Houghton Mifflin, 2003.

Silverstein, Shel. *Where the Sidewalk Ends, 30th Anniversary Special Edition: Poems and Drawings.* HarperCollins, 2004.

Novels Written in Verse

Creech, Sharon. *Love That Dog.* Joanna Cotler/HarperCollins, 2001.

Hesse, Karen. *Out of the Dust.* Hyperion, 1997.

Leithauser, Brad. *Darlington's Fall: A Novel in Verse.* Knopf, 2003.

Wayland, April Halprin. *Girl Coming in for a Landing.* Knopf, 2002.

Woodson, Jacqueline. *Locomotion.* Putnam, 2003.

PLAYS

If you want to write plays, it makes sense to read plays. You will learn much from studying how different playwrights solve problems of plotting, characterization, and other elements of storytelling on a stage. These are some of the successful plays written for children outside of the usual fairytales and adaptations from well-known stories.

Aiken, Joan. *Winterthing: A Play for Children,* illustrated by Arvis L. Stewart. Holt, Rinehart & Winston, 1972.

Alexander, Sue. *Small Plays for Special Days,* illustrated by Tom Huffman. Clarion, 2003.

————. *Whatever Happened to Uncle Albert? and Other Puzzling Plays,* illustrated by Tom Huffman. Houghton Mifflin, 1980.

Asher, Sandra Fenichel. *Across the Plains: The Journey of the Palace Wagon Family.* Dramatic Publishing Company, 1997.

————. *Blackbirds and Dragons, Mermaids and Mice.* Dramatic Publishing Company, 2003.

————. *In the Garden of the Selfish Giant.* Dramatic Publishing Company, 2004.

Jennings, Coleman, ed. *Eight Plays for Children.* The New Generation Play Project, University of Texas Press, 1999.

————. *Theater for Young Audiences: 20 Great Plays for Children,* foreword by Maurice Sendak. St. Martin's Press, 1998.

Mason, Timothy. *Ten Plays for Children: From the Repertory of the Children's Theatre Company of Minneapolis* (Young Actor Series). Smith & Kraus, 1998.

Zeder, Susan. *Mother Hicks.* Anchorage Press, 1986, rev. 1994.

————. *Wiley and the Hairy Man.* Anchorage Press, 1978.

NOVELTY BOOKS

The variety of these books sometimes reaches a level of such sophistication that they are not really for small children; they are often more suited to older children with an appreciation for their creative designs and delicate construction. For example, some pop-up books with pull tabs may be too fragile and complex for a toddler's small fingers to manipulate, but the intricate paper engineering may be part of the appeal for the older child.

Ahlberg, Janet, and Allan Ahlberg. *The Jolly Postman.* Little, Brown, 1986. (Letters tucked in envelopes from the mail bag.)

Big Dump Truck. DK Publishing, 2003. (A truck shape, with moving wheels.)

Cousins, Lucy. *Maisy's Pop-Up Playhouse.* Candlewick, 2003. (A pop-up dollhouse.)

Cruse, Howard. *Stuck Rubber Baby.* Paradox Press, 1995. (A graphic novel about coming of age in the sixties.)

Ernst, Liza Campbell. *The Turn-Around Upside-Down Alphabet Book,* Simon & Schuster, 2004. (Can be held in any position to read the letters.)

Hawcock, David. *The Amazing Pop-Up Pull-Out Space Shuttle.* DK, 1998. (A paper sculpture with movable parts.)

Kunhardt, Dorothy. *Pat the Bunny.* Golden Books, 1940. (Interactive touch-and-feel activities.)

Lacome, Julie. *Fingerwiggle Board Books.* Candlewick Press. (Fingerholes).

Marzollo, Jean. *Mama Mama/Papa Papa,* illustrated by Laura Regan. HarperFestival, 2003. (A flip book to read two ways.)

Munro, Roxie. *Doors.* Seastar, 2004. (Lift-the-flaps.)

Newell, Peter. *The Slant Book,* Tuttle, 2001. (A slant-shaped book with a story involving a downhill slant.)

Pinkney, Andrea Davis. *Shake, Shake, Shake: Family Celebration Board Books,* illustrated by Brian Pinkney. Red Wagon Books, 1997. (Encourages playing an African instrument.)

Schindel, John. *What Did They See?* illustrated by Doug Cushman. Holt, 2003. (It has a mirror at the end.)

Spiegelman, Art. *Open Me . . . I'm a Dog.* Joanna Cotler, 1997. (A book that is transformed into a dog.)

Stadler, John. *Take Me Out to the Ball Game.* Simon & Schuster, 2005. (Pop-up.)

Zelinsky, Paul O. *Knick-Knack Paddywhack!* Dutton, 2002. (Pull tabs with moving parts.)

INDEX

ABOUT THE AUTHOR

Barbara Seuling has had a long and outstanding career in children's books. She worked for major publishing houses as a children's book editor, wrote and illustrated more than fifty books for children, and has taught writing for children in college, online, and privately, as founder and director of The Manuscript Workshop. Her expertise in many areas of children's books makes her insights and advice for success invaluable to any struggling writer. She lives in New York City and also has a home in Londonderry, Vermont.

The information herein was current as this book went into production, but changes are inevitable before the next printing. Barbara's Web site will keep you aware of significant changes that are likely to affect children's book writers and publishers, so check it out periodically at http://www.barbaraseuling.com. If you have information to add, or have any questions about writing for children or The Manuscript Workshop that were not addressed here, you can reach Barbara by e-mail through the Web site or by regular mail at P.O. Box 529, Londonderry, Vermont, 05148.